FIX YOUR DAMN

How to Painlessly Edit Your Novels & Stories

BY JAMES OSIRIS BALDWIN

A Gift Horse Productions Book

CONTENTS

INTRODUCTION

This book is for writers who have finished a manuscript – a novel, novella, short story, or serial – and who want to self-publish their work or find an agent or publisher to get it on the market.

The fiction marketplace has never been larger or more competitive, and not just the indie and self-publishing space. Publishing houses are picking up more books than ever before, but there's been such a huge influx of new manuscripts in the last five years that literary agencies are literally being flooded with books – far too many books for them to ever be able to represent. As a result, agents and editors are increasingly picky about the books they select, while the 'slush pile' is being transferred to readers in the self-published book market and to websites like Wattpad and Tablo.

Self-publishing has become a liberating and viable alternative to publishing with a house, but it comes with a very real challenge: competition. If your

1

manuscript isn't at a level comparable to house-published books, you're very unlikely to get the positive regard and career you're seeking. There are exceptions, of course – there's poorly written, poorly edited stories littered all over the Web with numerous gushing comments – but it doesn't change the fact that those stories often receive more ridicule than praise and rarely go on to become commercial successes. They fade back into the sea of mediocrity that is Google without making any profit for their authors.

Market competition is creating demand for better quality manuscripts straight out of the gate. It's at the point where some agents are recommending that new authors get an editor to review their manuscript before they even send their first query letter. For self-published works, significant editing before publishing is now practically mandatory. This leaves new writers with three options: hire a freelance editor to work on their manuscript, somehow convince an editor to do it for trade of services, or self-edit their own work.

Editing is a professional craft which requires experience, skill, and most of all, time. Editing is a highly specialized profession, and because of that, editors are expensive – self included. Hiring an editor to edit a self-published manuscript is out of the reach of most new authors. Between $500-$1000 USD is typical: more, if your book happens to be in very bad shape.

If you're pitching your first book or self-publishing with no idea if you'll make a return on your work, those three zeros at the end of the price tag are intimidating. Even if you crowdsource, you still have no assurance that the money spent will matter. To put it in perspective, the average debut self-published novel sells less than 50 copies, and the average house-published novel often doesn't sell many more than that past launch day. Once you have a few titles (or an agent) and some success to push off from, it makes perfect sense to invest more money into editing, but when you're starting out, many authors have to go it alone.

If you're the type of person who wants to fix their own damn book, I wrote this guide for you.

MY STORY

My first novel was completed before I began my career as an editor. As an English Major, I knew some basic stuff about editing. You use editing to make a manuscript 'better'. You connect all the plot threads, fix up weak characters, try to make your first draft dialogue sound sharp. You do your research and get your facts right. If your character is named 'Sam' in Chapter 2, she better be named Sam in Chapter 13... so on and so forth.

I finished my first book in 2009, when I was in my early 20s. I was already an experienced freelance writer and making my living from writing, but I really had no idea what to do with this book. It was a 100K word monster that emerged misshapen from my sweaty brow, a mutated parody of an actual novel. I redrafted and agonized and sent my new rewritten chapters to my betas... and got nowhere. To be frank, my first manuscript was a mess.

Worse, I became codependent with my book. I was emotionally bound to my manuscript. I often wanted to throw it at the window or on the ground and jump up and down on it. You may also know this feeling, and the insidious, creeping horror that comes from realizing that this creation – which you slaved over for so many hours, which contains real pieces of yourself – is now something you can't stand to look at... Especially once the rejections start creeping in.

Not only did my book suffer, so did my queries. I made mistakes on several query letters, which I only spotted after sending them to literary agents... and I never heard back from many of those agents, not even form rejections. I realized that even when you're trying your hardest, if you don't know the tricks of the trade, there are mistakes which are nearly impossible to spot until it's too late.

Fast forward 6 years to 2015. I joined the editorial team for the Australian Journal of Dementia Care, a medical practice journal for people working in aged care and research, and spent two years there before moving to a large Australian not-for-profit organization. I now have four years as a staff editor under my belt and can successfully edit and polish my manuscripts to a professional level in about a month, including rest time. No drama, little fuss, no remaining errors of significance, and only one bottle of Baileys consumed. Well, maybe two. But not all at once!

I love writing, and I love a well-crafted and beautiful book. It is my hope that *Fix Your Damn Book!* will help you to successfully self-edit your novel manuscript, story, novella, or non-fiction book. This is not a book on how to write a novel, but will help you turn your manuscript into a polished work of art which you can send to agents or publish on Kindle with confidence.

Be warned: there's swearing ahead. I'm Australian, and we swear like pirates down here on the butt-end of the planet. If poop-related words offend you, this might not be the guide for you.

A NOTE ON SELF-EDITING

Just as representing yourself in court instead of hiring a lawyer is not ideal, neither is self-editing. I will say, baldly and without hesitation, that self-editing is no substitute for having a well-trained third party editor go through your work. You will never physically be capable of doing as good as job as that objective professional can. There are emotional and physical limitations of the human brain that will prevent you from being as good as someone else. This goes for me, too, even though I edit for a living. I usually hire an editor to go through my books once I am through self-editing them.

If you know what you're doing, you can be about 90-95 percent as good as that hypothetical professional editor, and for your first novels, your query letters, and magazine short stories, 90-95 percent will put you at the top of the slush pile. In addition, if you are a skilled self-editor and can do most of the work, you can probably hire a less expensive editor for copy-editing or more easily arrange a trade with another author.

All authors, regardless of whether they have an agent, must also know how to effectively self-edit before they turn their work over to a publisher (or readers, for that matter). You cannot turn in an unedited draft manuscript to your agent: they will send it back and tell you to edit it first. Sometimes, editors may request to see parts of your draft work or a synopsis, but they will expect you to refine your book as much as you can before it lands on their desk. The better a job you do, the faster their editing process is, and the more time they have to spend in discussion with you about the most important editorial considerations of your manuscript. It's also likely that they will make fewer changes, and you won't have to do as many rewrites.

If you have to hire an editor for anything, hire one for either developmental editing or line editing (or both!). You can most easily and objectively handle copy editing and proofreading yourself. Copy editing is the part which a lot of writers seem to fear the most – grammar, spelling, punctuation and basic formatting – but it's actually the easiest and most formulaic part of the editorial process. With practice, I believe it's possible to catch around 99% of copy editing errors without help. The bigger, messier steps are the hardest and most time consuming, and it can be extremely difficult to see outside of your own mental loops when it comes to a story. Copy editing is far more formulaic. Once you have the tools to know how to copyedit efficiently, it doesn't take very long to do it and do it well.

If you bought this book expecting to learn how to self-edit your work to be 'perfect', let's set it straight right now. True perfection is impossible. In fact, editing in general – while generally striving for perfection – uses a management framework which allows for a certain healthy margin of error. Even publishing house editors, who might work on thirty books a year and whose books are checked by colleagues, proofreaders, and the layout team, often have to publish corrections for books on the market which still contain mistakes. If this happens to you, it's okay. You will do better on your next editorial pass.

Once you begin to see success with your writing and have money which you can invest back into it, I recommend that you hire a third party editor and cultivate a good relationship with them, especially if you're self-published. If I was writing a series of books and my first book made $1000, I would immediately invest that grand into a good editor for the second book.

What self-editing CAN do is make your books good enough for market. 'Good enough' means that they will be accepted by the vast majority of your readers who will not notice any flaws that an experienced critical reader could possibly pick up, and that you will get few or no irritated fan emails correcting your spelling or punctuation.

PITFALLS AND CHALLENGES

In line with the above, there are a number of pitfalls to self-editing. These are a few of the many challenges which an author faces as they sculpt this solidified chunk of their imagination into something that other people will also enjoy.

Your helpless familiarity with your own work is a huge problem. In fact, objectively assessing your own work is a literal impossibility – the human brain cannot physically do this. In 2013, research by Maura Pilotti and Martin Chodorow at the Hunter College CUNY in New York confirmed something that editors have known anecdotally for years: it's way harder to spot errors in texts you are familiar with, versus unfamiliar texts. This has to do with the way that the brain adapts to patterns. Because you've been staring at the same words for months (or even years), your brain is used to the visual patterns in the manuscript, errors included. Your eyes skip over errors because there's no 'alarm bells' that go off as you read. Training helps, and there are some tricks to improve your ability to spot these invisible errors. We will cover these later in the book.

Self-criticism is another major issue. Most writers and artists are thin-skinned by nature. We invest a great deal of time, love, and effort into our work, and the worst fear of most authors is that their books are never read or loved by an audience. Combined with the pressure-cooker culture of the publishing industry and the intensely critical nature of editing itself, you can end up feeling pretty strung out. Like battery hens, many authors feel trapped by the publishing system and resort to plucking at themselves (or attacking other writers) to vent steam. I'm sure you can imagine – and have possibly already experienced – the particular kind of stress that comes about from picking relentlessly at yourself and your creative efforts. Self-sabotage makes self-editing practically impossible... not least because when you think you're doing a great job ("Yeah! I'll show you! Die, manuscript!"), there's a very good chance you're actually removing big chunks of the organic, passionate prose that defines your voice.

Have you ever heard of *style*, in the editorial sense? Style refers to a set of consistent editorial guidelines which can be applied to a piece of copy: the way things are capitalized, the way certain words are spelled, the way references are presented (if applicable), the way that footnotes, paragraphs, sentences and hyphens are formatted. Did you know, for example, that when laying out a book for publishing, it's standard practice to begin indents from the second paragraph of a chapter? You can see that formatting technique in this book, if you go back to the title of this section. The first line (and first paragraph) are not indented, because it looks strange if the title is against the margin and the first line just beneath it is not. Those kinds of details are things that you probably didn't notice while reading books as a member of an audience, but those little professional touches are important to agents and readers.

One of the biggest challenges with self-editing is that editing is, by its nature, a critical exercise. You're critically examining own work for problems and flaws. This is difficult to do. It can even be genuinely painful. We invest a lot of ourselves into our novels, stories, characters and the worlds we create. Bypassing our mixed emotions about our creations – the fear and exhilaration, the love and frustration – to objectively edit it is something you may not feel capable of doing, at first.

Good old-fashioned patience is another issue. A lot of people, while learning a new skill, don't do the activity for as long as they should. Patience isn't a talent or part of a person's nature; it is, by and large, a cultivated skill of its own. You can learn patience, and you have to learn to be a good editor. Many authors just want the book *done.* By the middle of your 100,000-word manuscript, the fatigue starts to set in, but impatient editing always results in significant errors. Impatience in writers manifests in lots of different ways: desperately wanting to show one of your best betas your barely finished first draft chapter one (which over-familiarizes them with the contents, reducing their effectiveness at later stages) to rushing copy editing and missing repeated words and double or triple spaces.

You MUST be patient, or willing to cultivate patience, to be able to do a good job. The less systematic your editing process is, the more you are likely to miss, and the harder it will be to address the weakest areas of a fresh manuscript: usually the middle sections. It also increases the likelihood you will have to edit your manuscript over, and over, and over again.

SO, WHERE DO WE GO FROM HERE?

From this point on, Fix Your Damn Book! is divided into seven sections.

- *First Steps*, which includes information on how to understand and approach editing as a skill-set, and how to frame yourself emotionally for the difficult task of criticizing your own manuscript;

- *Diagnosis*

- *Developmental editing*

- *Line editing*

- *Copy editing*

- *Beta-readers* and soliciting helpful feedback

- *Proofreading and publishing*

- In addition, there are four appendixes with stand-alone useful information on:

- *Appendix A: Writing and editing query letters*
- *Appendix B: Software for writers and editors*
- *Appendix C: Editing out sexism and special developmental editing questions for female characters*

- *Appendix D: A list of books I recommend to improve your editing and writing*

Depending on where you're at with your manuscript, you can use the steps outlined in *Fix Your Damn Book!* in any order, or read through it prior to your redrafting process and bear the information in mind as you revise. If you're happy with your draft and are just getting into the editing process, start at the beginning of this book and work your way through.

I highly recommend you supplement this book with a dictionary. There's dictionaries and good grammar reference sites online now – but please, for the love of spaghetti, leave off the thesaurus.

A caveat on editing as a set of 'rules'

Mention anything to do with 'rules' of writing and editing in any public forum populated by writers and editors, and you'll set off a bomb. "There are no rules!" some people cry, while others scream back: "Yes there are! And if you don't follow them, your book sucks!" Online conversations about grammar usually devolve into shit-fits and violations of Godwin's Law within a half dozen posts.

Unfortunately, as is often the case with explosive topics, both parties are kind of right. There *are* rules – especially when it comes to editing – but there are rules which can be broken, ignored or circumvented, and those which probably shouldn't be. There are rules which are accepted by most because they operate effectively. There are rules which are arbitrary and based on assumptions and opinions. Experimentation is part of the game in this regard, and anyone who writes entirely to a plan and a set of strict rules is going to risk producing some very dry prose.

> Add to the list from whence. Whence actually means from a place so when people use the term from whence you came they're saying from from where. It annoys me how many so called smart people use that the wrong way. Go back whence you came is the correct way to use the word.

Warden | Earth December 02, 2015, 4:54PM

> > Yes it is surprising how many people don't understand archaic English.
>
> GRW | Abbotsford December 02, 2015, 6:32PM

> A bunch of those words should just be scrapped and replaced with ones that don't confuse people. They sound derivative of words which in fact have quite different meanings. I'm thinking enervate, enormity, fortuitous, fulsome, luxuriant, noisome and tortuous.

Roger | December 02, 2015, 5:03PM

> I find most of the howlers in the notices we get from our daughter's school:
> "Incursion" to mean a visit to the school by someone - as opposed to an excursion...
> "explicit" rather than "specific"...
> Also there seems to be a total failure to understand gerunds:- "he objected to his going" (correct) instead of "he objected to him going"...
> I could go on...

TitusGroan | December 02, 2015, 5:04PM

> I disagree about number 19. He is wrong.

Figure 1: GRAMMAR FIGHT!

The point at which rules do become applicable when editing mostly has to do with comprehension. There are some fundamental rules of the English language and certain laws, which, like the laws of physics, can be depended on. You ignore them at your peril... Unless, of course, your work hinges on breaking those rules. Even then, it is worth knowing, understanding and accepting those laws first. You will find it hard to consciously circumvent something if you don't know the rules to begin with. Training is learning the rules, laws and norms of a discipline; mastery is strategically manipulating them to achieve a creative vision.

What's the difference between laws, rules and

norms? For example, if you typed BADS.LKJAYFH when you meant to say 'fish', you're screwing with the laws of English. No one will know that word is English. If you don't spell English with a capital E and call it 'english', you are not abiding by the rules which have been written into that language, but you're still intelligible. If you're breaking norms, you're messing with common standards which we mostly agree on as English speakers and readers, but which don't actually detract from the ability of your text to be understood. One of the best examples of breaking norms is the spelling of words in Net Speak, LOLcats and Doge memes. You know what the writer is saying, even if you don't agree with how they're saying it, but it has a subculture (and even a kind of grammar) of its own.

Everyone seems to have their own individual threshold where they draw the line. Some people really hate the idea that there's rules in language at all. For those of you who maintain that English has no established laws or rules, that everything is subjective, and that I'm a jack-boot wearing fascist, I challenge you to go to your local service station and order a coffee by gibbering random nouns at the attendant. "Sunshine! Order! Kittens!" Better yet, take a sign and write something like: *"!!OH COF YEAH LAATTTLL SKAJSKJAND boooon 1981238qd; ladsnk"* on it. See how far you get.

Getting a hang of the rules, laws and norms of English will help you communicate your vision. That's all they have to do. If that means you make a whole lot of stuff up or derive it from Russian or Chinese like Anthony Burgess, that's just fine, *as long as that displacement from the rules is what you want to communicate.* Most of the time, writers do not intend to confuse their readers. Even if you do want your reader to be confused, if you do it in the wrong way, they will get pissed off and your book will be thrown into the dustbin.

In no way do I intend for this guide to be an official instruction manual for becoming a professional editor or a singular guide to grammar and style. It will not teach you editor's shorthand, fancy squiggly symbols, or exhaust you with dictionary definitions and technical terms. *Fix Your Damn Book!* is not a style guide. That is not what this book is for. During nearly a decade of practice as a professional writer and editor, I've learned to edit in practical ways which produce a sound piece of copy in a decently short period of time, without excessive pain or stress. If you really want to know the proper names for grammatical functions, you can easily find them with the help of a dictionary or a manual of style.

For example, the definition of a run-on sentence in the Merriam-Webster Dictionary is formally: "... a sentence containing two or more clauses not connected by the correct conjunction or punctuation." Old Ironsides, the senior editor at the UK office of the magazine where I worked, had another definition: "If you read it aloud and run out of breath, it's a run-on sentence." In practical terms, she's right. In fundamental terms, what you're looking for is what the definition describes: a sentence that uses excessive commas, incorrect conjunctions ('and', 'but') and so on. Which of the two is easier to apply in practice? That depends on your personality and disposition, your preferred learning style, and your priorities. This book is mostly written for people who want a practical, easy-to-apply guide which they can keep by their elbow as they edit and refer to as needed.

In the spirit of the guide, this book is entirely self-edited. I wanted to demonstrate the kind of product you can end up with if you master the editorial process and work on your books yourself. *Fix Your Damn Book!* has been through same the process that is outlined in the next 200 pages or so, and if you're curious about how long it took, it was about six months to research and write (with a pause for a breakdown and half a year of full-time office work), but only about 4 weeks to edit and then send out to my betas.

If you happen to spot any errors and would like to (politely) report a correction to me, feel free to contact me at: fydb@jamesosiris.com.

FIRST STEPS

"There are three rules for writing a novel. Unfortunately, no one knows what they are." — W. Somerset Maugham

Editing is the point where you take a finished draft manuscript and turn it into a book. Editing is to writing what choreography is to dancing: a lot of repetition, a lot of planning, and a lot of work... all with the intention of making the end product look effortless.

Approaching editing without a sense of process and perspective is like trying to repair a broken down car engine without tools, training, or the ability to get into the car's computer. You can stare at the engine, wrench in hand, but unless you know what all the parts are and how to replace them or if they even need replacing, you aren't going to get very far in your efforts.

AIRPLANES AND EDITING: A METAPHOR

The US city of Seattle is the home of Boeing, the American plane manufacturer. Just north of Seattle is the city of Everett, which is home to the world's largest building, the Boeing Production Center. It is a single building the size of Disneyland, and is where every new Boeing plane is constructed by hand from a mixture of site-assembled and pre-fabricated parts. My favorite planes, the Boeing 777s, are assembled there by over 3000 people and several specialized robots over a two-week construction period.

Because every commercial airliner is still mostly made by hand, airline mechanics find themselves dealing with unique problems on each plane. To start with, every make of plane is different, and every plane of the same model – 747, 777, etc. – has its own needs, quirks and foibles. To maximize the safety and performance of the plane, the maintenance and flight crews have to be able to perform the routine general tasks which are common to every aircraft, but adjust to the individual aircraft they're working on. AVO-123 might have bombproof hydraulics but a fussy toilet vacuum system, while LKL-456 has one hydraulics backup system offline most of the time and an occasional cabin pressurization issue, but the bathrooms work perfectly. A skilled crew will be able to run standard procedures while adapting creatively to the machine, working with the particular configuration of their aircraft.

Novels are similar to planes in many respects. They are both complex structures held under functional tension by anywhere from 50,000 to 200,000 discrete, carefully balanced parts – in the case of a book, these are the words you've laid down to construct the narrative. Change a word here, switch a verb there, and you can turn your happy exclamation into a shout of anger. When you're writing, you're an artist: when you're editing, you're a mechanic. You are handing yourself a unique, hand-built artifact, and your job as an editor isn't to just generally 'make it good', but to tune it – like an engine – to achieve the goals you want it to achieve. These goals can be roughly divided into two camps: the semantic (the intended meaning of your sentences) and syntactic (the structure of your sentences). Semantic goals are aimed at making sure your writing conveys the story and characterization you want to show readers. Syntactic goals are based around making your writing sound good while you do the former.

The main difference between the amateur editor and the professional editor is the ability to suspend subjective impulses and act with their final semantic and syntactic goals in mind. To go back to the mechanics metaphor, an individual aviation mechanic might love particular aspects of a plane – maybe she really loves cockpit interiors and is an expert in resolving frizzled wires and strange air conditioning smells. But if she worked on those to the exclusion of other issues, there would be serious problems down the road. She might fix up the cockpit, look over the shiny Airbus 320 exterior, rev the engines a little and call it good. But if an overlooked rivet isn't in alignment in the hull or someone forgets to secure an engine casing (*cough* Spirit Airlines Flight 409 *cough*), the whole machine could fall apart. That's quite a serious problem, not least if you are a passenger on that aircraft.

Instead of allowing their subjective impulses to guide their trade, a professional mechanic will suspend her emotions and preferences. They will work both on what they're good at, and also on what they're not as good at. A mechanic tunes and evaluates with the end goal of 'what does this plane HAVE to do?' and works through their checklists methodically.

Of course, this metaphor only goes so far. No one is going to live or die by the decisions you make in your book, but your readers are, in a sense, your passengers. You are taking them on a ride, and editing is the set of actions you take to shape the nature of that ride. Is it smooth or bumpy? Is it long or short? When is it fast, and when does it need to be slow? Imagine a rollercoaster carriage climbing up a hill, rattling and clanking as it builds the anticipation of the descent. At the top, it teeters... and then plummets down, hits a corner, and jerks to the side as it hurtles towards the loop. It's dramatic. It's exhilarating. The rollercoaster track is a structure which is capable of telling a story.

The success of editing your book is partly based on your ability to respect, follow and sometimes bend procedures (namely, the rules of grammar, spelling, and composition) combined with the flexibility of working with your unique voice and tempo. It also depends on your acceptance that the narrative, at this point, isn't about you. It's about THEM, the reader. Your novel has a job to do. You may love that scene of your characters making stew in the inn's kitchen together, but if it doesn't do its job – which is to fly your readers' imaginations from Point A to Point Z – then it doesn't belong in your story.

REWRITING AND REDRAFTING

Now that we've hammered in that editing is a craft – and a blue-collar craft at that - I'd like to state that while self-editing and writing do blur into one another at points, there is a point of no return between the editorial process and the writing process. This point is usually around the time you start line editing. You might finish a manuscript, tear it apart, and find places where you need to add or rewrite sections. You then roughly edit those sections and work them into the manuscript before going back over the whole thing. This kind of patchy workflow is normal and natural.

However, once you have a complete draft, treat the editorial process as a slippery slope to publication. You should only start exclusively editing once you're fairly certain your manuscript is ready to ride that ride. Some people who have significant editing and writing experience are best served doing a progressive edit as they rewrite, but this is not true of most people.

One of the common questions I've seen bandied around in various forms is: 'how many times should I redraft my manuscript?' There are many opinions on this, from the cynical ('as many times until the story is good') through to the arbitrary ('10 times, no more or less') and the flagellant ('Until its perfect and you are as good as your favorite author!'). Unless you are a masochist who loves nothing more than a good session of self-administered mental and physical torture, there is absolutely no reason for you to edit your manuscript 10 times or more. Hell, there's no reason for you to have to draft your manuscript four times, let alone 10. I have no idea why any sane author would put themselves through double-digit redrafts of their manuscript... though on second thought, there actually are two very compelling reasons: anxiety, closely followed by its dark twin, procrastination.

Anxiety is not founded in reality. It might be inspired by past trauma, but anxiety is fundamentally illusory. Writers as a rule are delicate, emotion-driven creatures, heavily invested in their own work, desperate to be read and received well by an audience, afraid that they are not good enough or that their book isn't going to sell. The publishing industry exploits these needs ruthlessly, and it is very easy to misjudge your own work and become anxious. This is how writing, rewriting, editing and angsting can become a blurry haze which never ends, leading to three, four, five years spent on a single overworked manuscript. I know first-hand how anxiety greatly skews your own opinions of your work. It also effects the quality of your writing, especially when you are redrafting or rewriting while in an anxious or self-critical frame of mind.

Working with a manuscript is much like molding a piece of steel. If there's something wrong with it, you might be able to reforge it into a better product, but the more you mess with it, the more static and brittle the base material becomes. In other words, every time you redraft your manuscript, you cut the heart out of it just a little more. The more you revise something critically, the more likely you are to erase the moments of clumsy passion that motivated you to write that story in the first place. Is this a certainty? No. But I'd argue the risk goes up exponentially each time you rewrite and revise your single piece of work.

So the only answer to the redrafting question, in my opinion, is 'redraft and revise until the story is optimally compelling and entertaining'. Does the story make sense? Is it essentially well-written? Does the book have decent pacing and is fun and/or thought-provoking? If so, why would you want to redraft it another 25 times? Why are you seeking some kind of nebulous perfection your anxiety tells you it lacks?

Remember that your manuscript isn't actually a novel until someone publishes it – whether that be you or a publishing firm – and people start reading it. If it has no audience, your manuscript is a paperweight gathering dust in the drawer. If you're sitting on a manuscript that you're redrafting over and over again, you haven't finished your book. You're procrastinating moving into the completion phases – editing and publishing – due to anxiety, real or imagined fears of rejection, or a lack of perspective on how good (or bad) your work actually is.

The editor is the person who puts up the boundary and says: this is it. You have a book: now we're going to make it awesome. When you're editing your own work, that person is you. So revise and redraft your manuscript until you feel it is acceptable. Editing is the phase where you 'perfect' (and the term is used very loosely: no book is perfect) your manuscript into book form. You are ready to begin when your work is more-or-less logical, congruent (in other words, all the parts of the story fit together), the chapters are in the order you want, the characters say and do what you want them to say, and the story evokes the emotions you want it to evoke.

HOW TO DESTROY YOUR MANUSCRIPT

A problem arises when you invest too much of yourself into your book: perfectionism. The easiest and fastest way to completely destroy your manuscript is to edit in perfectionism mode. If you're stressed while editing, not only will you accidentally skip over errors, you'll lose your love for the book, and you'll also degrade the quality of your writing.

"But!" I hear the Internet cry: "Aren't we supposed to punish ourselves? Aren't we supposed to kill our darlings? Rip it apart? Put it on LiveJournal to be snarked? Shouldn't we hate our book and try and reform it until it is worthy of an agent's attention?"

The short answer is 'no'. No, you should not do these things. They are not healthy or objective ways to look at something you care about. You can be as snarky and hostile to yourself and other writers as you like, but taking a conflictual approach to someone's work does nothing but feed the high-strung negativity that is already an entrenched part of publishing. It is an attitude that has silenced the voices of many young writers, and that results in the repeated rejection of manuscripts that later go on to win awards and capture imaginations.

Imagine that your new manuscript is a puppy, around six months old. Or, if you prefer, a kitten. Something young, impressionable, and vulnerable. He is utterly dependent on your guidance to become a healthy, responsible dog or cat.

Now imagine your untrained puppy doesn't respond to the name you gave him. You know the puppy hasn't heard its new name before, but instead of sitting down with treats and patiently teaching him, you take him out behind the house and beat the shit out of him with a golf club, screaming at him for not coming when called. Needless to say, not only is that a really scummy thing to do, you will screw up that dog for life. And yet... this general approach is what an awful lot of writers do to their manuscripts and themselves.

Artists love to self-abuse. If you treat your manuscript as something made to be punished, you will warp it. If you treat YOURSELF as someone to be punished for writing an imperfect novel, you will warp yourself.

Editing is fundamentally a critical process, and it's inherently stressful to edit your own work. The ACT of editing is more than enough criticism for an artist to endure. I have to say that craft-of-writing books often drive this mentality. If you read agent blogs or agent books, you come away believing that every sentence has to be snappy, engaging, lean, fleshed-out, perfect...

Perfect.

In real life, the endless pursuit of perfection leads to nervous disorders: depression, anorexia, body dysmorphia, and all sorts of other problems. The pursuit of perfection will also destroy your fragile confidence in your manuscript. Perfection does not exist. Drum this into your mind-brain.

As you read Donald Maass's The Breakout Novelist or trawl Writer's Digest for tips and tricks, remember that the intense pressure – which originates from the publishing industry and which is policed by aspiring authors – has an awful lot to do with money. Agents are fussy and perfectionistic because their income is based on commission. They want the books they think will make them a lot of money. Sometimes, this is good writing. Sometimes, it's not. At the time of writing (2015), you're going to be hard-pressed to find an agent if you are writing anything other than young adult fiction. As far as the industry is concerned, that's where the money is: the Harry Potters, the Hunger Games, the Divergents. If you try to listen to everyone, write and edit to patterns, conform to genre trends or lists of features and formulas, you're going to end up with 100,000 words of McDonalds.

So really, the very first thing you do to successfully edit yourself is to relax into a positive frame of mind. Accept that you will not catch every mistake or end up with a 'perfect' book. You may come back after finishing your edits and further revise the opening paragraph, or change things after a number of rejections. You may even scrap the entire book for another project. But please, don't fall into the trap of beating your metaphorical puppy with a metaphorical golf club.

Once you've rested your manuscript, I want you to have a flip through and make a list of ten things which really stand out to you as good moments in the script. Look for moments that make you lift your brows and nod and smile. Even if these scenes DON'T belong in the final draft – and they may not – they're worth celebrating and hanging on to. In the Age of the Author Platform, those good cut-out pieces of manuscript are useful. Publish them on your website as Easter Eggs for your fans someday, or turn them into stories of their own.

SETTING HEALTHY GOALS

In the spirit of not beating yourself like an abused puppy, there are the kinds of goals which will help you move forward in your career, and the kind that lead to burnout and disheartenment. Here are some examples of both.

Bad goals:

- You want to get your book good enough for an agent.
- You want to publish it next week and you need to get it finished as soon as possible.
- You have a deadline in two weeks so you have to finish it in one week.
- You want to impress your mother/father/partner, who doesn't believe you can finish the book.
- You have to write 50,000 words a month or you fail as an author.

Why are these bad? These kinds of goals increase internal pressure and trigger stress responses. As I mentioned, it's nearly impossible to edit well while stressed. In addition, if you come to associate your novel with a state of anxiety, your brain will believe that this object is cause for concern. Once your brain does this, you basically develop a phobia. Working on a book when you are phobic of it inevitably results in procrastination and other avoidant behaviors (sudden fatigue, endless Netflix or YouTube, irritability) as you unconsciously try to escape the negative stimulus.

Instead, associate your book with rewards. These can be small material rewards, or just a pat on the back. Make your goals achievable and positive and you will see your energy surge.

Good goals:

- Edit Ch. 2 opening paragraph for cadence[1].
- Substantive edit of first page, then read-aloud.
- Copy edit 30 pages.
- Write beta checklist.
- Rewrite 1500 words of Ch. 3.

There's a few reasons these goals are good for you. Firstly, they're achievable. Secondly, they take the drama out of the exercise. If you're sitting there having a panic attack over how awful your first paragraph is, you'll freeze up. If you assign a particular focus to your editing – editing for cadence, or sentence length, or to get the main character's name into the first line of Chapter One – you feed your brain with a measurable goal.

Set yourself goals which are attainable in the time you have to edit. If you have two hours, you should set one or two goals. If you have a day, try seven. Studies have shown that that your memory is capable of holding a maximum of seven short pieces of information in the short-term, so seven or fewer goals means you can keep them all in mind as you work through and complete each one.

---

[1] *Not sure what 'cadence' is? Don't worry. We learn more about that later on.*

DEALING WITH SUBJECTIVE PERSPECTIVE

Even if you follow my advice in the next chapter (Diagnosis) and leave your manuscript in a drawer for six weeks, the fact remains: You wrote the damn thing. Familiarity interferes with editing, but familiarity is unavoidable when you're self-editing. If you have the ability to split your mind into separate personalities and your other personalities happen to be editors, you have a distinct advantage. Everyone else has to learn to view their manuscript objectively. Here's some of my tips for gaining that distance:

- If you're in love with a particular scene or chapter, pay special attention to it. There's a pretty good chance it gratifies a part of your ego or a personal fantasy. This isn't necessarily a bad thing, but it requires you to step back and ask yourself: *"Is this scene something other people can relate to, or does it just please me?"* If the answer is that it only relates to you – your desires, your sense of self – and not people at large, you will need to rethink that scene or rewrite it with your audience in mind. You may love math or politics, but if the climax of your book is ideological instead of personal, you will get canned. It is likely that you'll have to do less work on this than you'd expect: it's usually a case of cutting some exposition or waffling, and adding in some action and emotion.

- Pay special attention to the scenes that you hate for the same reason. Why, exactly, do you hate them? They're not always as bad as you think.

- After finishing each chapter, sit for a couple of moments and ask yourself a single question: "What happened?" Did everything in that chapter add to the story? Was every scene in that chapter a building block for the climax?

- You may love your slice-of-life scenes between characters, but they probably don't need to be there. This is somewhat genre-dependent. Romance can get away with this more than thrillers can, but if they don't build the story, if they don't build the tension, cross them out. Eating, toileting, bathing, sleeping, dreaming (yes, dreaming) and other mundane things rarely need to be left in a manuscript. Sometimes, they do, but that's because they serve a dramatic function. *Jurassic Park* has a very notable toilet scene, for example.

- Draw a big red box around anything your eyes skim over, or that makes your eyes tired. This is a huge red flag for slow prose or needless description, exposition, or dithering.

- If you can do it, imagine yourself as a strange reader picking up your story for the first time. What does the first page and first chapter seem to be about? Is it the story that you intended to write?

- Be kind to yourself and your voice. It is very easy to 'whitewash' your own writing. One of the marks of an inexperienced editor is the inability to appreciate and recognize style. As mentioned in First Steps, some things are rules (like putting quotation marks around dialogue), and some things are norms. You want to preserve your voice. Good editing will not touch your writer's voice, but will instead tune your style so that it shines.

- Read everything aloud. Everything. Titles, chapter headings, everything.
- Resist the urge to ask others if the story is 'good' at this stage. Positive or negative opinions can sway your perception of your own writing, especially if the person is very close to you. Give the book to your First Reader after the developmental stage, and you'll get more out of their feedback.

THE FOUR-STEP PROCESS

There are four stages of editing which are done more-or-less sequentially. Different editors call the steps different things and split the process at different points, but I refer to them as the Diagnosis, Developmental Editing, Line Editing, and Copy Editing stages. Some people include 'proofreading' as a distinct 4th or 5th stage – I don't. The reasoning is that I consider proofreading to be a bit of a given, and count it in the post-editing follow-up phase which also includes beta reading.

Diagnosis

Sometimes referred to as 'pre-reading' or assessment, or the 'read before you touch it!' stage, I prefer to call this stage 'diagnosis' because the true hands-off reading approach never worked for me.

Diagnosis involves a notebook, a plot planner, and 3-12 hours of time, depending on how fast you read and how long the manuscript is. What you do here is read with an eye for large, macro issues and generalized problems, which you jot down as you work. You will also make your first round of 'queries': the critical questions you ask to examine your plot for holes, flaws, inconsistencies, and similar problems. Queries have to be ruthless. Why do you have a race of cat people? Why is the goal of the protagonists so important? Is it Tuesday or Wednesday? Why does the queen eat baked beans for breakfast instead of pancakes? Queries are the questions on the gaps you must fill.

Diagnosis is also an appropriate point to note and fix critical, obvious issues which will make the next stages of editing difficult: but only things which can be done quickly. For example, if one of your characters suddenly changes names, you can change it through your entire manuscript at this point.

If you start diagnosis, try and see it through. Even if you realize your manuscript is not yet ready for editing, you'll finish your plot planner and synopses and have a good idea what it is that needs work. Instead of flitting back and forth and fixing parts that go on to break other parts, you'll have a well-organized, well-labeled manuscript that you can use to work through a fast redraft. You will have to step back from Editor Brain and re-enter Writer Brain if this is the case.

Developmental editing

Also called 'content editing' or 'substantive editing', the developmental editing stage is the hardest and longest part of the editorial process. This is where you must pick through your plot, characters, book structure, chapter beginnings and endings, and create order out of chaos. If you're a 'pantser' – someone who writes with little or no planning beforehand – this step is often extremely painful. For 'plotters' who have a pre-existing plan, it can be a bit easier... but not really much easier. Around 50% of your time spent editing will likely be spent on this part of the process, which is certain to include some backtracking and rewriting.

The trick to effective developmental editing is to break your manuscript into chunks. However, not all chunks are created equal: there are places where you can reliably break up your story, and parts which should be edited together. The chapter on developmental editing is where we will learn where to split your manuscript for the best experience.

Line editing

Technically an extension of developmental editing, line editing is where you focus in from your semantic editing onto the syntactic stuff: the structure of sentences and paragraphs. You've wrangled your plot, executed a couple of unnecessary characters, and sobbed over the horrible death of your favorite descriptions. Line editing is where you tighten each individual scene and chapter, check your dialogue, and, most importantly, fine tune your cadence. You add in all of the micro changes which the developmental process unearthed. You check over your new rewritten sections, make sure everything sounds the way you want it to, and then move on. This is also the point where I recommend you do your first read-aloud, and line editing while reading aloud is a great technique to improve your writing at the word and sentence level.

The Importance of Cadence

Poetry inclines itself more naturally to expressions of cadence, but it is really important for prose as well. In the Line Editing section, I will show you how to create and edit cadence to elicit particular emotional effects in your writing.

Copy editing and proofing

Copy editing is your fine detail work. This is where you look at your manuscript word-by-word, checking for spelling, grammar, word repetition, formatting, editorial style (distinct from writing style/voice) and other similar issues. Once you've picked through everything and fixed all the nitty-gritty problems, you proofread to check a second (and third) time. This stage of editing is quite technical and can be a bit dry, but if all has gone well, it should also be the fastest part of the editorial process.

The fifth elements: formatting, read-alouds and beta readers

Diagnosis, developmental editing, line editing and copy editing are the four steps in the self-editing process, but there are three very important final steps before you hit the publish button or send your pitch off to your favorite agent. You have to format your manuscript for submission or publication, you have to read the whole thing aloud and listen to it being spoken, and you have to run the finished product by some beta readers.

By the time you've started editing, you should be

lining up your betas. There are three different kinds of beta readers that we will look at towards the end of this book, and you can employ them for different stages of the editorial process. The short version is that there's first-step betas (who read your manuscript just after line editing), second-step betas (who read your manuscript after you have made revisions based on first-step beta feedback and after copy editing), and your First Reader, who is a trusted person you give your entire finished manuscript to review at different stages, depending on need.

STYLE GUIDES

A style guide, also called a manual of style, is a set of standards that an editor uses to style written documents in a consistent way. Style guides provide uniformity in style within a document and across multiple documents. The focus of style guides is usually on copy editing – the fine detailing and formatting of a document – but they typically also include loose guidelines on content as well.

There are some very well-known and venerable manuals of style – *The Chicago Manual of Style* and *The Oxford Guide to Style* come to mind – and if you want to edit to a professional, widely accepted style, those two are a good place to start. You can pick up copies of various commercial style guides or subscribe to them online. Some of the most common manuals of style are listed at the end of this chapter.

Besides the 'big' style guides, like AP and *The Chicago Manual of Style*, there are also 'house styles'. Nearly every publishing house and magazine has 'house rules' which the editors on that team know to use. In the *Journal of Dementia Care* team, we had rules like: 'No period after letters in contractions like 'e.g.', 'Mr.' and 'i.e.'. That was the accepted style for that magazine. We have a manual, which I helped to create, and which is now being used by the next generations of editors working for that publication. If you're sending your work off to a publisher, they will further edit your manuscript in their company's house style. Don't be offended if they change your shit around.

If you're self-publishing and plan on publishing more than one book, you'll be well served by developing your own style guide or referring to an established manual of style which is from your country of publication (or the country of the audience you're most concerned with). This will provide your readers with a consistent, professional level of editing which they will come to recognize as part of your brand. It will also help you to more efficiently edit your current and future books.

The style I've developed for editing manuscripts is specialized for longer works of narrative genre fiction, particularly the fantasy/sci-fi/urban fantasy genres. It focuses on the qualities which are generally demanded by agents and audiences in the current decade: fast pacing, consistent tense, snappy dialogue, and logical temporal sequencing. The copy editing style is roughly based on the Chicago Manual of Style, and advice on punctuation and formatting is derived from standard manuscript formats (such as the Shunn Format) and from what I have observed in trade and mass-market paperbacks.

If you find yourself disagreeing intensely with any of my firmly stated advice – "Perfect tense is evil! 'Smiling softly' doesn't make sense! Don't use bold for anything except headings!' – I recommend you cross those things out, research an alternative, and write it in the margin to develop your own style. Styles are not the same as laws of a language, and if you have a love affair with adverbs (like Patrick Rothfuss), you could still get lucky with a publishing deal and a squillion-dollar advance (also like Patrick Rothfuss). I always flag character tangents, for example, but readers of Stephen King and writers like him might love character tangents. You may not flag something of that nature if you're trying to write like Stephen King, but bear it in mind as being a possible style issue as you work.

STYLE GUIDES FOR ENGLISH-LANGUAGE GENERAL PUBLISHING

Here's a bunch of different 'official' style guides. The following are ordered by country:

Australia

Style Manual: For Authors, Editors and Printers by Snooks & Co for the Department of Finance and Administration.

Canada

The Canadian Style: A Guide to Writing and Editing by Dundurn Press in co-operation with Public Works and the Government Services Canada Translation Bureau.

EU

Directorate-General for Translation (European Commission). *English Style Guide*. The European Union.

UK

New Hart's Rules: The Handbook of Style for Writers and Editors by Oxford Press.

USA

The Elements of Style by William Strunk, Jr. and E. B. White.

The Chicago Manual of Style by University of Chicago Press.

The *AP Style Guide* is also well-known in the USA, but is more useful for journalists than it is for novelists.

Style guide abuse is a real possibility in editing, and if you're the sort of person who likes to reference a prescriptive style, be aware that style guides, as static documents, are there to do precisely what they say they do – to GUIDE. You must also in part be guided by the creative passion that drove you to write a novel in the first place. Your muse and your inner taskmistress or master must work hand-in-hand for you to become a successful self-editor.

DIAGNOSIS

Now that we've covered the headspace part of editing, it's time to begin! Sort of. Because the first step of editing is to let your bouncing baby manuscript rest in a drawer or desktop folder, untouched, for anywhere between two and four weeks. Yes, really - no looking, no touching, no nothing. If you already started messing with it or recently read it through, you may need to rest it longer – closer to six weeks.

This step is practiced by many successful writers for a reason. Resting your manuscript before you get into editing has many, many benefits, not limited to but including:

- Resting puts enough time between you and your writing to ensure you've become somewhat unfamiliar with the words and can read it with less bias.
- It ensures you'll look at the work with fresh eyes. If you're too used to staring at the errors on the page, you'll miss many of them when

you try to copy edit.

- By resting, you disassociate yourself from what you have written. It doesn't hurt as much to cut it up.
- Your brain has time to percolate on some of the ideas and thus can flesh them out more.
- You can immediately see simpler and clearer ways to convey your messages.
- You can finally remember details that you wanted to include but couldn't quite put your finger on during the draft phase;
- When you reengage with your book, you gain a deeper feel for what works and what doesn't.

So rest. Take a break. Work on another book, if you're some kind of masochist, or on your author platform (your blog, Twitter, Facebook... whatever your drug of choice happens to be). If you're one of those power pulp-writer Indies, you should generally have a couple of books resting as you draft your current work. Come back to the rested manuscript with fresh eyes. Your editing will be far more effective after you've taken a vacation.

After you've rested your manuscript, it's time to get stuck into diagnosis: working out what, if anything, needs to be re-written or replaced in your book, and making a rough assessment of what you need to do in the developmental and line editing stages.

Diagnosis is derived from the Greek word for 'discernment', the process of understanding the operation of something. Diagnosis is used in many different disciplines, mostly ones that deal with complex systems: medicine, computing, mechanics, and editing.

As you work on your story, you are looking for the symptoms of weak plot, characterization and lapses in tension, as well as problems with lack of detail or conflicting details, among many other things. Passively reading through your manuscript is good for getting a refresher on your work, but without some critical reading and organization, the other, more difficult parts of editing will drag.

There are many different ways to organize your manuscript. One way (and the method discussed in this book) is to 'chunk' your book into sections. By working on a single chunk, the length of the manuscript becomes more manageable. It's easier to pay attention to each section of the story, in the early stages.

To begin diagnosing your manuscript, here's all of the things you will need:

- A hard copy of your manuscript, formatted for editing;
- One colored pen for corrections. Red is the standard, but really, use any damn color you want;
- One writing pen (blue, black, purple) or pencil;
- Your first list of daily goals;
- A Plot Planner (coming up in this chapter);
- A fresh exercise book or comp book;
- A desk or table. You need a large space to spread your manuscript out at first;
- Your synopsis or summary notes;
- Colored tabs or post-it notes.

Then, do whatever it is you do to feel safe and focused at your workspace. Shut the door, grab your coffee, pet a kitty, dress up in a business suit: whatever gets you in The Zone. I personally recommend no kitty (lovely as they are, they tend to lie on things), chewing gum, headphones, and shoes. Yes, shoes. Putting my work shoes on helps me focus when I'm working at home, for some reason.

FORMATTING A MANUSCRIPT FOR EDITING

You can do a fair bit of editing on your computer screen, but at some point, you will benefit from a hard copy pass of your book. While creative software is rapidly catching up in most areas of digital media, you still can't get the kind of hands-on ability to sort, pile and mix that paper offers. Even younger people who have grown up paperless will find that a hardcopy manuscript is beneficial at the developmental and copyediting stages. Screens subtly fatigue the eyes over the course of a day.

Formatting at this stage doesn't have to be complex, but it does need to facilitate editing. I use a 1.5 inch left hand margin, size 12 font in a *different font to the font that I drafted in*, double spacing, and page numbers. At this stage, it doesn't matter if you indent first lines or add spaces between paragraphs. Leave a wider margin than you usually would for submission (standard manuscript formats usually call for 1 inch margins all around) so that you have room to write notes.

If you're very new to formatting, here are the steps to follow to arrange your manuscript:

1) Set either your right or left margin to 2 inches. This depends on your personal preference and handedness. Remember that this copy will be printed out to edit by hand, so choose the side which feels most pleasant to write on.

2) Select everything in your document. Set your line spacing to 2.0 or 2.5. If you have spaces between paragraphs, leave them. If you don't, make sure to use the page or paragraph settings to add a bit of space in. You need enough room to be able to write notes.

3) With everything selected, change it into a pleasant, easy to read and print-friendly font. I really like Arial for non-serif and Constantia or Georgia for serif, but any easy-to-read font will do. Don't get too fancy: you'll be staring at these pages for a long time. You should use a font different to the one you've been writing in to help freshen up your eyes.

4) Make sure to add page numbers! Header or footer, it doesn't matter.

5) To separate your chapters cleanly, insert page breaks at the end of each chapter. If you haven't finished a particular chapter in your first draft manuscript, find the best point in that area of the text to add in a page break.

If you don't know how to add page breaks, here's how to do it in OpenOffice or LibreOffice:

Put your cursor at the end of the last line of your chapter, then go to the main menu and click Insert > Manual Break. A little dialogue box will come up. Don't change anything: just click okay. A dotted blue line should appear at the bottom of your page, chopping off any of the text beneath and forcing that text to the next page.

To add page breaks in Microsoft Word, go to Layout > Breaks > Next Page.

Page breaks ensure that your chapters begin on a new page, eliminating the issue of Chapter Two starting on the same page Chapter One ends. It's pretty damn difficult to work on chapters if you can't put them in piles. You'll end up cutting pages in half!

Don't feel pressured to format your manuscript for publishing or submission at this stage. Setting XML for .epub and other ebook files is an art, and format for paperbacks even more so. Just work with a format that is neat and comfortable for you to use.

SUMMARIES AND QUERY LETTERS

Editors and agents want plans and synopses, query letters, and blurbs. These sadists demand that authors condense their 200-500 page labor of love to three pages, then one page, then half a page, then a single paragraph, and then a sentence (your pitch or logline). While this is extremely inhumane, there are several good reasons why agents and editors expect you to be able to do this, and do it well. The most important of these reasons is that readers need these butchered summaries of your book to decide whether they want to read it or not. The callous, overworked agent who wants a query and synopsis is actually pushing you to do something very important. You have to be able to tell people what your book is about, and quickly.

Start your query letters and back-cover blurbs, log-lines/elevator pitches, and other oppressively short summaries now. Yes, now: months in advance of ever actually firing one off to an agent. Days ahead of beginning a comprehensive edit of your novel. While you're resting your book, you can be working on your summaries and query letter.

A query letter is essentially a business letter combined with the back cover blurb that you would like to see on the back of your novel. They should be short, professional, and interesting. Queries are very difficult to write: along with the log-line, they can take as long as a full novel draft to refine and perfect. For a brief guide, check out *Appendix A: The Dread Query.*

A synopsis is a 1-3 page summary of your central plot. It is used to efficiently recount the main story line (and maybe one subplot) in a straight-forward, unembellished way. The synopsis is a formal document type, which means that – like a business letter or essay – it has rules and a standard format that is expected by those who ask for one. A 3-page synopsis is a 3-page synopsis, not a 7-page synopsis or a rambling spiel with liberal use of 'I wrote it this way because...', and if an agent specifies that they want a 1-page or 3-page synopsis, they are not realistically going to make an exception for your novel.

A log line is a single sentence that should capture the heart and soul of what your story is about. It is quite often the hardest task an author faces when they're thinking about pitching and selling their book, but it is your front line summary. When people want to know what your book is about, you have to be able to tell them.

Here is the logline for my debut novel: *"A Russian mafia hitmage must save a unicorn who has come to New York city to head off a galactic cataclysm."*

And here a differently framed logline from Twitter that got several publishers and agents requesting full drafts to read:

"Kick-ass gay wizard hitman fights God-destroying virus. Car-chases, casino shootouts, and criminal magic."

Blood Hound is quite a complex story, with two main plot threads and a couple of subplots, but this is the core story that I am trying to tell. It's not terribly elegant, but the heart of the book is there. You know what it's about in either case... they are different retellings of the same core story with different emphasis.

I recommend that you practice creating loglines for published books that you know and love. Try it on other people's novels a couple of times if you've never done this before, and eventually, the process of skeletonizing stories to look at the bones will begin to come more naturally.

When you're writing summaries and promotional copy ('copy' being marketing jargon for a text document), there's six elements to focus on: characters, situations, objectives, setting, antagonists, and decisions.

Characters

People read stories because they involve interesting people doing interesting things. What defines interesting? Sympathetic, flawed characters with the potential for growth, of course.

This is easier if you have one character, naturally. However, some very good stories have a cast with two or three focal characters. *A Song of Ice and Fire*, for example, has three in just the first book alone: Ned

Stark, Daenerys, and Jon Snow.

But what about the other perspective characters in *A Game of Thrones*, you may ask? If you examine the book from a structural standpoint, you will see there are three main plots which could feasibly stand alone as their own books. Bran's story (at this stage of the series) could not stand alone, though as he progresses over the series, his sub-plot becomes more independent and he gains the status of a protagonist. But if you took out Ned's chapters, they'd form a contiguous novella of their own. Same with Dany. Same with Jon. If you've written an epic fantasy/sci-fi with these multiple POV and multiple keystone plots, pick the most important one: the one which is the spine of THAT particular book. In Game of Thrones, that would arguably be Ned's story. All of the other plot-lines continue on to other books in the series, but Ned's perspective is the one which has a defined beginning and end within the one book, and which acts as a catalyst for all the other stories in future books. Even though Daenerys' story takes up a good chunk of the book and is perhaps the central character of the series, she is not the central character of this particular novel. If you were writing a summary of a book of similar complexity, the focus of your synopsis would be on the Starks.

If you're writing a series, this is a good time to begin work on a series synopsis or 'series bible', if you haven't already started one. While your editorial task is this particular finished book, it is good to have this factual short-form material to refer back to and add to as you work on the next books in that particular series.

Situation

What is the backdrop against which your main character operates? This is not a description of the world-at-large: it is the world which your focal character interacts with. The local world.

CSI: Miami, for example. Just from the title, we know where this particular crime show is set. If it was *CSI: America and Canada*, we'd have an awful lot of explaining to do before we arrived at a crime scene in Miami. YEEAAHHH.

You may have developed a very intricate world, but for the purposes of a synopsis and query, only the environments which your focal character interacts with are relevant.

Objective

Sometimes phrased as: "What does your character want, or want to avoid?" Also known as 'the stakes'.

Goals aren't necessarily straightforward. The ones that matter aren't so much related to the events of the story, as they are related to the reasons why your protagonist participates in these events. The true objectives of your protagonists are based on their flaws and the things they need to overcome those flaws. In the first half of a book, protags are generally trying to achieve an objective which allows them to continue on as they are. A proud character will try to preserve their dignity; a fearful character will give in to their fear and want to run away. In the second half, they generally begin trying to achieve objectives that will allow them to master their flaws.

Externally, what is your character really focused on? In *The Hunger Games*, Katniss Everdeen doesn't want to have anything to do with Panem or their gladiatorial arena. What she wants is to protect her sister, and to survive the ordeals which she must face to ensure her sister is never subjected to the Games. The tributes from the more martial districts, the ones who fight to volunteer? THEY want to win the Games.

If your focal character isn't striving for something, you have a problem. You must identify what it is you want them to attain or avoid.

Antagonists

Antagonists are whatever stand between your protagonist and their objective. Antagonists aren't necessarily people. In The Hunger Games, it is the Games themselves which disrupts Katniss' desire to survive. Behind that lays the antagonistic society of Panem. All of the individuals and circumstances that cross Katniss's path are her antagonists.

Systematic opposition is one kind of antagonist. However, opponents who have agency (the ability to act independently) typically make for the most exciting antagonists in fiction. The crime and thriller genres are basically built on that entire concept. Who or what is your character up against? What is trying to stop and impede them?

Following on from the above, *why* is the antagonist or opposing force trying to stop your character?

Most stories are built on disaster: the avoidance, fulfillment, or aftermath thereof. What is the worst thing that happens, or could happen, in your story?

Decisions

What decisions do your characters make, or have to make, to avoid or overcome the situation they're in? The Decision-Objective (or Decision-Goal) partnership is one of the primary ways a writer drives conflict.

These things – Characters, Situations, Objectives, Antagonists and Decisions – are the basis of your ideal synopsis, synopsis, query letter, log line and Twitter pitch. "Daenerys, a shy princess under the thumb of her tyrannical brother (character, antagonist), is married off to a foreign king (situation). When he perishes, she must rally herself and her new people (objective, decision) and seize her birthright before a race of undead warriors (antagonists) invades her homeland."

THE IDEAL SYNOPSIS

Summaries, synopses, log-lines and queries are for your potential agents and audience: The Ideal Synopsis is for you. The Ideal Synopsis is a synopsis you write before you really crack into editing, which gives you a strong, descriptive summary of what you *want* your book to be about. You had a vision when you started this novel. Whether it was a vague vision or a solid one, now that it's been written, it's time to ensure that the book is telling the story you want.

Creating the Ideal Synopsis is a two-stage process. During your first big read-through, note down all your major plot points and write a rough synopsis. It doesn't have to be of good enough quality to send to an agent, or written to any standard format, but try to keep this first synopsis fairly brief and unornamented. This synopsis should be a literal blow-by-blow summary of everything that happens in your story, in the order you wrote it. If you have a very complex plot or multiple viewpoints, you may find that this first 'synopsis' draft is better suited to index cards or post-it notes. This is your draft synopsis.

Then, take that draft and, in a new document, use the information to write your Ideal Synopsis. This is the synopsis which corrects any continuity errors or fills in any gaps you noticed while writing out the draft. Write down the events of your novel as you think they should be. Look back to your draft synopsis and see if any of your plot threads don't resolve, or if any of your characters are superfluous or weak. This should be a three-page summary of what you want your story to be at its very best.

The Ideal Synopsis is a good exercise because it gives you a broad overview of everything that happens in your novel. It gives you documents that you use to answer that extremely important question: "What's the story about?"

I really do think it's better to get these short-form pieces down on paper in some form *before* you begin editing your manuscript. Short form summaries force you to distill your work, to cut out all of the fluff and dithering and really pin down what your story is about. The process of doing so is maddening and frustrating and sometimes very painful, but it is an incredibly valuable learning process. The resulting documents are what you can use to guide and steady yourself as you edit and revise, and will also help you to write your query and blurb. It will also help you to create your plot planner.

CREATING A PLOT PLANNER

Different people have different kinds of intelligence. Some of us are very linear, dealing best with neat reams of notes, books laid out in sequential order, and a logical presentation of information. Some of us keep our clothes on the bedroom floor in 'clean', 'worn once or twice' and 'dirty' piles, and treat our novel outlines in much the same general fashion. In either case, you are writing a novel – which readers have certain expectations of – and if you want to be published, your book has to embody a satisfying dramatic structure.

Yes, this does sound like laying down rules. But just like a three-course meal, there is a structure and a purpose to the structure which is important to recognize. Entrees are light by design, so as to 'lead in' to a main course; dessert tends to be the richest course, to leave guests with a pleasurable afterglow of fullness. Dramatic structures do the same thing, but for the mind.

There is a lot of creative license within the novel format... but even the most whacked out books still embody a dramatic arc, even if that arc is chopped and changed and left intentionally unsatisfied as a kind of artistic statement. Effective artistic statements are within the realm of the masters – and the masters use structural outlines. I have heard down the writer's grapevine that some Famous Authors say in public that they do not use outlines, but that is an omission of fact. Literary agencies and publishers almost universally require their authors to submit the outlines and/or synopses of their upcoming series ideas before they write them. These documents are reasonably flexible, but they're still outlines.

To help your manuscript and your other short and long-form copy (blurbs, bios, summaries, etc.) form a cohesive whole, you need to see the cloth you've woven into your novel at a glance. You need to be able to see the patterns you have woven into that cloth, and that is why you need a plot planner. Some people's plot planners are huge outlines – some people use a couple of pages of dot-point scene notes. No matter what your plan is, it is your guide and your friend. When you're blind, it will help you see. If you somehow managed to draft a book without one, you need one to self-edit your book afterward.

There are any number of ways to create this particular document. It can be a work of art unto itself or a dirty notebook full of dot points. Karen S. Weisner's wonderful book *First Draft in 30 Days* gives a very comprehensive outline plan that works well for some people, especially when they are first conceiving a novel. Because you're likely working from retrospect, your plot planner is to help you keep track of what's already there and to help you identify what still needs work. The following sections detail two types of plot planner I like to use: one is very linear, and one is more spatial and visual. I shall give them the brilliantly creative names of Notebook Plan and Wall Plan.

The Notebook Plan

To create the notebook plan, you need the aforementioned notebook (I personally like large, unlined sheets, like an 8 x 11 in sketchbook), a packet of cheap colored markers or markers, a nice writing pen, and a basic in-head knowledge of your plots and subplots. The two synopses you wrote (the draft and ideal) will be helpful. You will basically pick a color for your main plot and one for each subplot.

As you read your manuscript, write down a one-line summary of the plot progression within a given scene. Put a colored circle of the appropriate color beside the descriptions you write. An entry might look something like:

Chapter One – Beginning of Beginning

First Line: Establish Agent Jones at the murder scene.

First Scene: AJ notes the dead werewolf has been shot, the bullet removed and not found at the scene of the crime.

Subplot 1 (different color): Agent Knight arrives: romantic rivalry begins.

That example is hideously simplified, but you get the gist: detail the interlinking plot streams and make sure each one is complete and in order. Your goal, with this exercise, is to make sure that each plot and sub-plot has a beginning, a middle and an end, and to ascertain if each one of those plots and subplots has an emotionally satisfying rhythm. The beauty to this method is that you can very easily identify the rhythm you need: just fill in the blanks!

The plot planner will also show you where your plots need to be tightened. This exercise is effectively the cure for a saggy middle section, something we will expand on that in the developmental editing part of this book.

The Wall Plan

Similar to the Notebook Plan in all but execution, this

is for the more visual/spatial thinkers among us. Take a large sheet of butcher's paper – the kind you buy on a roll – or a whiteboard. Make it as big as you like. Tape it to a wall large enough to deal with this monster. I prefer my paper to be about 1m wide x 1.5m long.

Then, draw this funky scar-shaped figure on it, from the bottom left corner (right if you're left-handed), to the top right corner, leaving enough room around it to write:

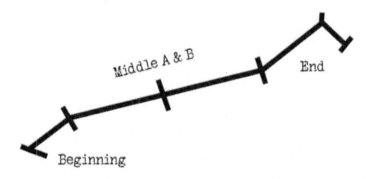

Middle A & B

End

Beginning

Instead of markers, you may want to use a bunch of different colored pens. Essentially, though, each one of those points on that line represent the key moments of your main plot. Fill those in if you know them well. Otherwise, fill in those and your subplots at their appropriate place on the line. The subplots should each have their own color, and they should also create seven circles each, weaving in and out of the original main plot structure like strands of a braid.

Both of these are very effective. I often use both: the notebook plan for all plots and subplots, the wall planner for balancing the main plot and primary subplot (sometimes romance, sometimes not). If you turn up with big gaping gaps of colors in your plans, you know your subplots aren't being paced as well as you could do it. All of your subplots should either tie up, or provide a cue to demonstrate that the sub-plot will be picked up in the next book.

Other alternatives to these two include mind-maps (linked bubbles in streams), a wiki (I have a desktop wiki for LILIUM and The Alexi Sokolsky series that I use to collect and sort all of the world-building and plot information), drawings and spreadsheets, or just a bullet-point word document if your brain works that way.

If you're the sort of person who thrives on practice, and you want to have a go at creating both of these before you tackle your own manuscript, I highly recommend giving it a go with your favorite Young Adult book. Why YA? Because YA tends to have plots which are sufficiently complex to be engaging, but simple enough that you can do the exercise more readily than you could with something as sprawling as *Lord of the Rings*. It will work with any book you know well and love, though. You will soon see what an intentional work of art these novels are.

Movies are also great for this exercise. Try breaking your favorite film along a wall planner for practice. Such exercises often lead to a 'Eureka!' moment for young authors.

CHUNKING AND MARKING CHAPTERS

I love the word 'chunk'. It sounds so... meaty.

Chunking will help you edit faster and better than you otherwise could. How you chunk is up to you, and depends in part on how your book is structured. The following is my recommended method for three-act manuscripts, the most common sort in genre fiction.

Assuming your manuscript conforms to a three-act structure, the (ironically) logical way to break it up is to separate it into four sections: Beginning, Middle A (first half of middle), Middle B (second half of middle), End. Then, you divide each chunk into its component chapters or scenes.

If your story structure is more complex, and/or you have multiple points of view, it may be easier to chunk your book into point-of-view sections first, then by act (beginning, middle, end). If you're a smartypants who wrote some kind of non-linear narrative, then you're also smart enough to figure out where your chunk-lines are.

Once you've done this and have your chunk piles, grab your colored tabs. Pick one color for chunks, and one (or more) for chapters. If you're a relatively tidy writer, you probably have clear chapters marked out in your manuscript, so add your first set of tabs at the beginning of each chunk, and then mark every chapter. Now you can quickly flip from chapter to chapter through the bulk of the manuscript. If you're not a tidy writer, this is a good time to work out where your chapters should begin and end. I hope you followed the line breaks tutorial earlier in this book, or you're in for a hell of a time.

By the time you start editing, your manuscript should have strongly defined chapters (or scenes, or books – however you've chosen to divide the text). If they don't, you need to work out why. Occasionally, you get a manuscript which is tricksy and that has some gaps or chapters which could be placed in one part of the book or another. Sometimes, you have a mostly-finished manuscript that is missing bits you know you need to write in. If this is your issue, mark them out as well as you are able to, get to rewriting, and then come back to editing. Find the places you think do or will culminate in a chapter. The next part of this exercise, separating the book by sections, will help you define where those peaks and drops of tension really are.

Now that you have your chunks and chapters marked, use your summaries to maintain an overall perspective on the story and refine each section individually. You can keep an eye on the macro-scale view of your novel by referring to your synopses and planner.

We will look into these chunks in-depth in the next chapter, Developmental Editing. For now, use them simply to break up your reading as you make your first diagnostic scan of the text.

THE DIAGNOSTIC RUN-THROUGH

Some people may have the ability to imagine themselves as another person and read through a manuscript with complete objectivity, but I am not one of those people and I don't know anyone who is. Instead of pretending that you can be completely objective about your own work, I believe it is better to read with certain broad critical elements in focus on your first reading: macro-crit, for lack of a better term.

So take your chunky, well-tagged manuscript, and read it from beginning to end with these things in the forefront of your mind. Make notes, tag pages, winnow out troublesome scenes or chapters and set them aside in a special needs pile, but focus primarily on educating yourself on the manuscript from an editorial perspective. Keep your plot planner close and progressively fill it in as you read.

Here are some sample questions you might ask yourself as you assess each part of your book.

Plots and sub-plots

This is where you will lean heavily on your plot planner. Mark and track each one of your plot threads, and assess them separately and in conjunction with one another to work out which are strong and healthy, which are weak and fixable, and which must be culled from your book.

- Are the plots *congruous*? In other words, do the events of the story flow naturally from one place to the next?
- Do the scenes of each plot make sense in context of the overall narrative?
- Are the events sequential? (Even if your book has a non-linear narrative, ala. *Pulp Fiction*, the events of each plot will still need to be able to be viewed sequentially)
- Do the plots interconnect properly? As Donald Maass wrote, plots are often at their most powerful when they suddenly converge at crucial moments.
- Identify the main emotional peaks of your plot. Do they feel unbalanced, as if the tempo of the story was skewed somehow? Most authors tend to make their plots bottom heavy (too much at the end) or top heavy (at the beginning), and are inclined to neglect the middle or let it waffle on.
- Do you ever lapse into 'everyday life' scenes?

Cooking, cleaning, toileting, grooming animals, playing with pets. Step back and ask yourself if this is what a reader unfamiliar with your characters would want out of a story in your genre. If so (and there are some stories which get away with this), how can this scene build tension and suspense instead of snuffing it out?

- Are there scenes missing?
- Are there scenes that don't work?

Pace

- Are there points where your story tempo lags?
- Are there points where it moves too quickly for an unfamiliar reader to follow?
- Do your eyes skip over any sentences or scenes? They're probably too abrupt, or too long-winded.
- Do you feel physically tired while reading a particular section or scene? As above.
- If you haven't finished a particular scene or haven't ended it cleanly, check it for pacing. It's possible you said everything you needed to say too fast, or tried to expound on something which could have been done a lot quicker and given way to greater conflict. Battle scenes and sex scenes are surprising culprits for ruining pace (see inset).
- Do you have cathartic (emotional) moments?
- Are actions easily predicted? Unpredictable actions by characters creates suspense.

Characters

- Make a list of characters. Does each character have a purpose in the story?
- Does your protagonist make significant

decisions?

- Do they enact those decisions? If not, why not?
- Do minor characters add color and flavor to the setting, or are they merely transactionary?
- Do your feature characters achieve their goals, or lose out on their personal goals (willingly or unwillingly) for the ultimate story goal? Either can work well, provided you clearly delineate their fate.
- By contrast, do any of your characters 'peter out' or fade away, never to be heard from again? This is a critical error to flag and fix.
- Do your characters have unique presence? Do they speak differently from one another, even in small ways, or do they lack voice?
- Pay special attention to your antagonist: what are they doing in each chapter/scene/chunk?

Once you've sorted all of this out, your printed manuscript should be bristling with post-it notes, sticky tags, circled paragraphs, and other assorted marks, crosses and large red symbols. Congratulations! Now it's time to get your wrench and begin the developmental editing stage.

DEVELOPMENTAL EDITING

"I want to communicate... that editing is shaping and creating writing as much as it is something that refines and polishes it. I want to step away from all the energy spent on separating editing from the writing process, shoved off at the end of it all or forgotten about altogether." - Jeff Anderson (Everyday Editing, Stenhouse, 2007)

Developmental editing will be what takes up most of your time, along with line editing, and indeed the two will blur into one another at points. Add in spontaneous rewrites, and you have quite a job on your hands.

Diagnosis has given you an idea of what you need to fix: now, you will find yourself revising scenes and stitching together loose subplots. The bulk of your work is found in your first-pass developmental edit, and this is why we chunked the manuscript. You'll be working with small sections of book and your plot planner. If you found some problem chapters while you were reading through and splitting your manuscript, deal with those separately. Sometimes, you may need to split a chapter into individual scenes if you have some especially knotty problems or want to focus on a theme or catalytic event.

Developmental editing is editing for plot, characters, and setting, voice, congruency and cohesion. To be honest, there's a lot of rewriting at this stage of editing. If you're wanting to study up on writing, I recommend the following books:

- *On Writing* by Stephen King. A magnificent book. Even if you're not a Stephen King fan (I'm not) this book is full of absolutely invaluable insights into writing as both an art and a profession.

- *Techniques of the Selling Writer* by Dwight W Swain. A classic book on writing as a craft, it is still as relevant today as when it was first publishing in the 70s.

- *From 2K to 10*: very helpful advice for getting more out of each writing session, as well as advice about making your plots more congruent.

- *Invisible Ink* by Brian McDonald: one of the best books I've ever read about capturing the theme at the core of a story.

- *The First 50 Pages by Jeff Gerke*: excellent, practical, sometimes scathing advice on sharpening your first crucial three chapters.

I recommend these books due to the improvement I saw in my own work and the work of others after reading and studying them. If you have to only pick one, I'd suggest *Techniques of the Selling Writer*. Swain really knows what the hell he is talking about.

With the basic structure and your plot in mind, we'll get stuck into the guts of what makes a good story, starting with one of the most elusive concepts in fiction: voice, and how an author can edit their manuscript to showcase it.

FINDING AND IDENTIFYING YOUR 'VOICE'

'Voice' is a term that describes the unique ways an individual writer can apply language to their writing. This can be as subtle as the way they use conjunctions (and, but), through to the words they make up to describe things. Voice can be choppy, lyrical, flat, sharp, or purple (as in, purple prose). It can literally be any combination of qualities, which you, the author, build into your composition. Voice is not what you're writing about, but *how* you are writing it. It is somewhat interchangeable with the word 'style' (e.g. Neil Gaiman's style is lyrical, Stephen King's style is efficient and tense), but the word 'style' indicates a certain intent that 'voice' lacks. Style is the flourish of color that you swirl at the end of the brush stroke; voice is the way you hold the brush and paint in the first place.

This is why 'voice' is rarely defined in how-to-write books. It's hard to define and harder to explain, because what makes for 'good' voice varies from person to person. Beyond some trope conventions, no one can predict what makes an author's voice 'good' or 'bad' in the eyes of an audience. During the writing stage, voice is something that is very instinctive and subjective... but like everything in writing, it is a *skill.* What some people dismiss as a 'talent' is in fact a skill that has been practiced and studied, over and over, until the practice has become innate.

Self-criticism and critical feedback from others can easily leave a writer feeling uncertain. You may mistakenly erase your voice while trying to edit something to be 'better', or vice-versa. Conversely, if you're emotionally invested in your work, you may feel very defensive about the sections of your manuscript which you regard as being exemplary of your voice and resist the efforts of yourself and others to rewrite, edit or omit them.

This is a capital reason that Internet forum feedback is rarely helpful to authors. You know the trolls I'm talking about: they're usually relative strangers who earnestly 'correct' a great many things that don't actually need to be corrected. Authors frequently receive 'critique' from unsolicited parties who have read their work and feel the need to stamp their own ego on it. The Internet, by its relatively anonymous nature, allows people to shoot their mouths off without fear of social repercussions. Online writing communities can often be very helpful, but you can also get well-intentioned help from people whose own writing is not up to your standard or whose voice is very different to yours. Sometimes, their 'advice' or 'feedback' is quite negative, and can be driven by egotism rather than expertise. The best feedback tends to come from those who are at a similar level of success and skill to yourself, wherever that happens to be. If you're looking to improve your voice, find a place where you are the youngest and least successful writer in the chatroom, put your pain aside, bare your writing, and listen.

Many unskilled amateur editors will try and suggest improvements based on how *they* would write it. If you listen to these people, you'll end up gathering anywhere between five and twenty opinions on how your book 'should' be, and it's easy to get bogged down in a cycle of self-criticism and uncertainty. Lack of self confidence in this regard can make determining your own voice a stressful exercise. If you don't erase your voice, they will.

But the question remains. What *does* makes for good writing, and good voice?

Good writing is any writing which is *congruent* and that does not have significant grammatical or syntactic errors. 'Congruent' means 'to be in agreement with' or 'harmonious'. When writing is congruent, it agrees with the basic rules of English, in that it is readable and comprehensible, and all parts of the story mesh together well. If all parts of your book are congruent on the macro and micro scale, your writing is already *good enough*.

Voice should also be congruent, in that your voice will consistently shine through in your book. However, appreciation of an author's voice is intensely subjective. Millions of people love Stephen King's style and voice: millions of people hate his books and his voice. No one can deny that King is prolific, professional and dedicated, but a lot of people still don't like his novels. They dispute his talent, not because there is anything wrong with his work, but because fiction is a matter of taste... so looking for 'good' writing, past a certain point of technical ability, is not very realistic. What you *can* do is edit for congruency, to make sure that your voice is consistent and recognizable to those who do like it, and who would like to see more of it throughout this book and the others you write in the future.

IMPROVING VOICE

At the broadest level, screening for congruence focuses on the plot, character/s and setting of your novel. Then you have screening at the *semantic level*, where you make sure your words mean what you think (and want) them to mean. Generally, most writers have good ideas for plot and characters. Semantic voice issues are what many of my clients want to improve, in terms of developing their own skill.

Here is a semantic form I often see amongst amateur writers:

"Vampire Hunter Johnny B strolled down Main Street in his black trenchcoat smoking a cigarette. The tinge of his Marlboro Reds was in his mouth. He looked over the seedy bars and wondered where he would find his next job."

Here we have a bland introduction, the sort that was (and unfortunately still is) common in online text roleplaying. The passage is descriptive, and technically 'correct' in all syntactic ways, but it has no character and no discernible voice, emotion, or immersion. It's not as simple as 'telling vs showing', either, because even if you try and show, you're probably still going to bore the shit out of your readers.

So let's first look at what the author wants to tell us:

- Johnny is a vampire hunter (who smokes).
- He's in a city or town with a seedy Main Street locale.
- He is down on his luck. He needs work and money.
- He's thinks he is (or actually is) a badass.

Let's assume the author is skilled enough to have thought of an overarching conflict to this story. Regardless, they cannot seem to effectively communicate the tension from the start. The moments of potential conflict – there's lots of things that could be happening to a vampire hunter down on his luck in a nasty part of town – are never realized.

At no point does the writer of a passage like this ever actually *evoke* the things he wants to show. He can only *narrate* them as if he was describing what he really wanted to write. The emotions, sensory impressions, tension and setting are obliterated in the attempt to press the necessary information on the reader. We have no sense of personality or place, and that indicates a lack of voice.

To develop their writing ability further, the author of the Johnny paragraph must *evoke* and *immerse* instead of *explain*. They could focus on smell or other senses. They could start with Johnny's thoughts, make them orderly or abstract, dark or optimistic. He could notice signs and the people that make the area seedy. Instead of strolling down Main Street, he could wake up in a dumpster covered in fang marks. The writer could write in an odd, lyrical style that indicates that Johnny is not from the modern era, that maybe he's older than he seems... or maybe he could write in the short, choppy sentences and hard tone of a New York gumshoe. The possibilities are endless. Voice is the difference between the same scene as painted by Monet (soft, pastel and impressionist) and Salvador Dali. It might be weird or lyrical or surreal or abstract, but it is never 'wrong' as long as it's there. For it to be there, you must cultivate it through a mix of observation, practice, and refinement.

Poor writing is the textual equivalent of a child's stick figure drawing. However, even the greatest artists start with stick figures when they begin a painting (a structure called an armature). Treat your unedited work as an armature and build it up from there.

THE THREE-ACT STRUCTURE 3: SON OF THREE ACT STRUCTURE

Pretty much every book on writing ever dwells on the importance of the three act structure. It's been done to death, but there's not much I can do about it: in the world of modern global entertainment, the three act structure is still the current modern dramatic form. It's not going anywhere any time soon, either, and any writer worth their salt has to know it inside and out.

Even if you're familiar with the three acts and confidently apply the structure (or subvert it) in your own work, some parts of it bear examination from an editorial perspective.

Three-act stories have a beginning, middle and end, which means the three act structure really entails a set-up, a series of cascading, increasingly serious disasters, and then a climax as the protagonist triumphs over evil... or doesn't. Everything from that point on is a denouement, the literary equivalent of a post-climax cigarette.

The three-act structure persists in non-linear narratives and narratives with multiple points of view. Sometimes the end is at the beginning, or there is a prologue or a chapter cuts into an in-media res scene. Some books are completely whacked out in terms of structure, assembled from the cutting room floor like *Finnegan's Wake*. In any case – especially in the kind of fiction that tends to sell at market – the three act structure is omnipresent. Other narrative structures do exist – see *Alternatives to the Three Act Structure* (p. 43) below.

The beginning sets something up. It makes something move. What is a story trying to set up? The end, of course. The key to an effective beginning is that it must contain the seeds of your future climax. The other thing with the beginning of a book is that, ideally, it is also its own three-act story. A skilled writer can do three mini-acts in the first chapter.

The middle section is also its own three-act structure. The beginning of the middle is the end of the set-up. Protag has committed to action; Antag is realizing that they have some upstart trying to stop them from achieving their goal. The middle is where everything must fall apart, one scene at a time. It culminates in climactic awfulness, sometimes called the Darkest Moment. Obi Wan Kenobi is killed. Harry Potter is alone and defenseless with Voldemort. Your protags are driven back against the edge of a bottomless pit. Woe and gnashing of teeth ensue.

The end has a special structure of its own. The protags recoup (beginning), discover some kind of will to succeed within themselves (middle), and then press forward to a final climax in some kind of emotionally satisfying way. In what way? Whatever suits the story best. The tense last scene is quite critical, however, and its resolution is the difference between your reader squeaking with glee as they read, and putting your book down with a grimace.

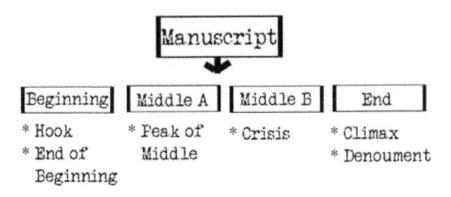

An overview of editorial chunks

We will be working through developmental editing chunk by chunk, with your planner and synopses to guide you. This guide has the chunks in order, but they can be assessed in any order. If you have one section of book that is more problematic or generally 'rougher' than others, focus on that chunk first. Energy is a finite thing, and is best spent on the tasks that make the biggest impact.

CHUNK #1 – THE BEGINNING

The beginning is where your key plot and sub-plots are introduced, along with characters, setting, and root conflicts. This chunk is generally around 30-50 pages long. If it's considerably longer than that (say, over 70 pages) and your book is not over 120,000 words, you need to revise this chunk and ensure that it has sufficient pacing and suspense. The length does vary somewhat by genre: thrillers and mysteries tend to have shorter beginnings; epic fantasy tends to run long.

You need to ensure that the reader knows what this book is about from the very first sentence. The beginning must also begin to set up suspense. What is suspense, exactly? The best definition that I have found was from Karen Wiesner, who defines suspense as: "[The] uncertainty over the outcome of a character's action."

There are two major key points to identify in your beginning.

The beginning of the beginning: first lines

Also called the 'Hook'. This section comprises that crucial first paragraph, first page, first five pages, and first chapter. The beginning of the beginning amounts to the first 5-10 pages of your manuscript, and is generally your shortest section.

Many books on writing talk about a 'hook' without ever really elaborating what a 'hook' really is. The hook is the sentence or paragraph that sets up the first conflict and initial suspense of your story. Imagine you are weaving a braid – someone's hair, or strips of leather – and instead of holding the first strand taut as you fold the others over and around, you just let it hang. One of two things happens: the braid falls apart, or it has an ugly loose bulge at the top and the person whose hair you're braiding gets annoyed because it hurts and pulls and feels uncomfortable. This is equivalent to what happens when there's no tension in your first line and paragraph.

Some people try too hard to capture their hook. They end up turning their first sentence into a kind of sales pitch. These kinds of hooks are usually obvious even to the writer of the novel. Rather than thinking of it as a line to sell someone on, try thinking of it as a promise you're making to the reader. The opening to your book is you saying to the reader: "This is what this book is about." If it is something like: "John stepped out of his car and put his sunglasses on," then what are you promising with that? Not really a whole lot. A guy named John is doing something mundane. Ho hum.

Or: "It was raining, water pounding the pavement. The moon soared high overhead." That's nice writing – you can't fault the prose itself, the cadence, or the mood – but it's not a fantastic opening line because other than a wet night and a full moon, it's not promising the reader anything.

But what about: "The rain pounded the pavement, the moon soared overhead, and the Hunt was in full swing."

The writing's not incredible, sure... but what's 'the Hunt'? What outcome does it have? We can assume, given the opening line, that this is what we're going to be reading about. You've just made your promise.

Your first paragraph is your second promise to the reader. It expands on the first line in a similar fashion to the above.

Here's another example. First line: "I woke up on the operating table, tube still down my throat, and all of the surgeons were dead". A mini-mystery is always a promise of something. In the rest of the paragraph, we learn that the doctors around our point-of-view character appear to have been dead for decades. The mystery promised in the first line deepens precipitously – and that's a hook.

This hook/promise thing is really important, and is why most novels beginning with dreams do not fly well with audiences and agents. Dreams are a false promise. "This is what the book's about!" and then: "Oh, no its not." If your novel starts with a dream sequence, consider rewriting it and moving the dream to a later point. If your novel begins with someone stepping out of a car, consider rewriting that, too. If you have an opening line with ominous weather, rethink it. What is someone or something doing in that ominous weather? A darkly dressed man with no umbrella and no sign of irritation, walking down an alley in piss-pouring rain is more interesting than the ominous rain and the storm itself. The same goes with dreams. If you open with a dream sequence, what is going on in that character's life (or about to happen) that incites the dream? See if you can start with someone really doing something.

In some longer stories, the 'hook' may actually be a standalone prelude followed by a chapter which sets up a new thread of tension. George R.R Martin uses prologues to good effect. A lot of agents say they hate them, but that's mostly because they read a lot of lousy prologues – not because prologues are inherently bad.

You have 15-20 seconds to keep someone interested when they first pick up your manuscript. If you're hoping to score an agent, the first five pages are what most agents judge your work by, assuming they get past your query email. If you're self-publishing, this section is the crucial start of your sample, by which most readers will decide whether or not they want to buy the rest of your book. Very few people doubt that the beginning of a book is the most important part, and it begins from the first sentence.

According to Jeff Gerke (author of *The First 50 Pages*), agents and editors are likely to refuse books which have weak first lines, lack an engaging hook, tell instead of show, contain point-of-view errors, start the main action too soon (yes, this is possible!), go into flashbacks or dream sequences at the beginning of story, and – the big one – lack conflict or stakes.

So, let's unpick those issues. Examine your first line with your editor hat on, and see if it does these things:

- Does it introduce some kind of conflict, or potential conflict? Inner or outer, it doesn't matter.
- Does it introduce character, a player in the story?
- Does it establish a sense of place or an immediate context?
- Does it somehow establish a hint of your voice or style?
- What is your promise to the reader?

Your first sentence ideally does two or more of these things. If it does all five, well done. If it does none of the above, you're going to have to rethink it.

The beginning of the beginning is where we meet a person (or people) doing something interesting, preferably something that partly defines them as a character. A detective is detecting, a killer is killing. A bad or challenging thing happens in some context; the protagonist/s must respond to the bad thing, which starts a chain reaction of shit they must commit to facing over the course of the novel.

Beginning of the beginning: first scene

Many new writers start their book with a scene that runs sort of like this: Jimmy the Protagonist gets up in the morning, eats his cornflakes, goes outside and goes to school, where he learns he's a ninja or something like that. In theory, this kind of slice-of-life to world-of-strangeness progression can be effective. In practice, it is a rare writer who imbue this kind of mundane scenario with enough subtle tension to be effective.

Imagine, for a moment, that a new Batman film comes out and the screenwriter decides that 'setting up' means showing Batman before he puts on the bondage suit and cape. If the first ten minutes of the film was Bruce getting his breakfast in bed while he reads his mail and reviews his stock portfolio, we probably wouldn't be particularly interested in the rest of the film. The fun only starts when he eventually puts his latex trousers on, brushes his teeth, and moves on to kicking ass. For this reason, you are unlikely to ever see Batman brushing his teeth, unless he's got two black eyes and is bleeding from the mouth.

As is often the case, books written 50-100 years ago were able to get away with this more. Before the Internet, the fictional lives of other people were things of interest to readers, who lacked multi-media entertainment and had more tolerance for stately prose. In the age of Snapchat and Netflix binging, mundane life actions tend to drag, especially near the start of a novel. Later on, they can be used to good effect to create sympathy and preclude tension, but not in the beginning.

Edit to ensure your first scene delivers on the promise of the first line. An effective technique is to highlight an action with an uncertain outcome, and then play out the uncertainty. If your protagonist is being pursued (first line), they duck around a dark building, jump a fence, and crouch in the shadows while dogs bark in the distance (first scene). The suspense comes from the implicit question: will they be caught?

The end of the beginning

The end of the beginning is generally where your story launches into a new phase, setting the protagonists up for the journey ahead. "You're a wizard, Harry!"

A story which I really got into is the RPG videogame *Undertale*, by Toby Fox. It has a very defined 'end of beginning' where your character literally passes through a door, leaving the relatively safe ruins area to enter a strange, dangerous underground. This is an idealized example of what the end of the beginning does: it moves your character from the relatively comfortable or familiar circumstances of the first 50 pages into an unfamiliar and challenging world. In a romance, it's often where the lead character meets and fails to impress (or be impressed by) the love interest. In thrillers, it's often where the protagonist learns about a horrible murder or other event of significance.

The end of the beginning should progress naturally from the first line and first scene. At the beginning of *Star Wars: The Force Strikes Back*, Luke Skywalker ends up with a problem that takes him away from his aunt and uncle's farm, and when he comes back, they have been murdered. He commits to avenging them. That is the end of the beginning.

CHUNK #2 – MIDDLE A: FIRST HALF OF MIDDLE

This chunk deals with the section between the end of the beginning and the middle of the middle. If this is your first book, you may also want to separate the chapter or scenes that comprise the peak of the middle into their own small chunk, so that you can compare it to the beginning and end.

Beginning of the middle

The first half of the middle is where your characters have been launched into their new world and are feeling it out. Some instructors and guides to writing say that this point is where your characters should relax, get to understand and accept their new world, and move on towards the second big point of climax. I firmly disagree. The end of the beginning has launched your characters into a new world, and the first thing they need to do is develop some goals – short-term goals to deal with the sudden shift in their reality. Your heroine has been arrested: her goals probably relate to getting free. Your hero has learned of a murder most foul: he spends a few pages strategizing how he will wring information from the few clues he has. Your protagonist has probably just had something difficult happen to them at the end of the beginning, and they're not going to kick back and play around with Secondary Love Interest while Primary Love Interest is tapping their foot and staring from across the other side of the ballroom. When Ned Stark gets to King's Landing in Game of Thrones, he doesn't even have a chance to sit down and have a stiff drink before a rain of royal shit falls right on his head.

The other challenge in this section is *setting*. You sketch out a setting and tone for your novel in the beginning, but the first half of the middle is where you have to reveal the intricacies of that world and paint it out for the reader's inner eye. The big trap which some authors tend to fall into here is that they get so into scene-setting and characterization that they lose all of the tension which they built up in the first part of the book. I call this 'Saggy Middle Syndrome'. You will want to make sure that you don't segue into forest wandering, stew eating, nose picking or off-topic, meandering conversations in this section of the book, while painting enough of the setting to really ground the reader.

Saggy Middle Syndrome at this point of a novel is *very* common in epic fantasy. Like... very-very. Nearly every fantasy book that has been delivered into my sweaty, twitching hands has this problem just after the heroes have made their commitment to the plot. You turn the page, and suddenly everyone is on horses, walking in the forest, cooking pots of stew or hunting deer or something. Don't do it. If you have any scenes like this, chop them mercilessly. They are a jungle from which readers and agents will not escape.

Another common plotting mistake at this stage of a novel is letting the characters off the hook. If you're writing a romance novel where your heroine has just divorced her shitty husband and is driving out to the country town where she will meet her new lover, have her zone out on the road within a couple of pages and hit a deer or something. Then she gets a lift from a trucker and arrives not having slept, and at the truckstop where she slumps in to have breakfast, there he is: the future love of her life! But... she smells like a cattle truck and has messy hair and has a split lip. He thinks she's some crack-ho that the trucker picked up and hates her on first meeting because his mother was a crack-ho and he has PTSD flashbacks. Suffering ensues, and readers love to watch protagonists suffer.

- Keep the tension simmering somehow, even if you need to explore other parts of your world. Have whatever happened bubbling ominously on the backburner.

- Ruthlessly prune content that slows down your pace.

- Develop other characters, setting and sub-plots, but have them somehow be in contrast to your main plot.

- The long hand of the antagonistic forces, whatever they may be, should begin to be visible in some respect.

- Have you preserved your voice after your energetic beginning? Is the voice in this section *better* than in your beginning? Go back and change what doesn't work in the beginning, but works in the middle.

Peak of middle

The middle of the middle is your story's turning point. It's generally a trigger for the direct involvement of the antagonists. A key murder. Learning who the real antagonists are (or who they might be) after multiple red herrings. A friend is kidnapped and the stakes suddenly get more personal than before. This entirely depends on your story, but around this point in the book, the reader should have a pretty significant O.M.G moment. Something happens to make the pursuit of their goal more compelling, raising the stakes. Perhaps they attain their initial objective, only to discover it causes an even bigger problem which they must then solve.

This is often a key 'twist' point. It is also where you can rhythmically set up an event which goes on to provide a bigger twist at the end of the story. The peak of the middle is usually only one, sometimes two chapters, but it can even just be a single scene within a chapter. Generally speaking, it's a relatively small section of book. It is, in my opinion, the hardest part of the book to write (along with first scene and the Beginning of the End).

One trick is to use this point in the book to show the audience what happens if the hero doesn't achieve their goal. The antagonist bombs a subway tunnel and gets away with it, but it's only a prelude to his bombing all of the train cars if no one stops him. Quick, get the hero!

This is the point where the antagonists begin to take significant, pointed notice of the protagonist's efforts, and may seek to specifically thwart them. An effort by the antagonists which leads the protagonists into a trap is a fairly classic example. You will have to recognize the needs of your own plot.

INTERLUDE: HOW TO FIX A SAGGY MIDDLE

After starting a novel, most writers begin to struggle around the 25000-to-30000-word mark. The reason for this is because the vast majority of authors have a good sense of the beginning of a book, a reasonable idea of the very end, and hardly any notion of what should happen in between them. We improvise until we finish, and then have to fix those sad, droopy middle scenes to keep the tension high.

As mentioned, the beginning of the middle should be a tense time, even if the narrative deals almost exclusively with interpersonal tension between the characters. Introverted or extroverted as your plot may be, white space after the end of the beginning is one of the few visual media techniques which is NOT also useful for novels.

If you have a trail-in-the-forest scene that goes longer than a couple of paragraphs, either condense it down or get rid of it. Same with anyone cooking, flying a spaceship, taking apart and polishing their guns for an excessive length of time, cleaning, eating in a restaurant, or driving down a long highway. These scenes are so common in early manuscripts (and unedited or poorly edited self-published books) that I can practically recite the tropes.

You don't have to sacrifice character development and interaction. Let's take an 'eating at the diner' scene. Go and look up the beginning of Pulp Fiction with Pumpkin and Honey Bunny. If you make Pulp Fiction a linear film by rearranging the scenes, you will notice where this scene comes in Jules and Vincent's story. Remember, however, that Tarantino has the ability to create 'white space' on his stage (the film set) with visual and audio stimuli that a book cannot do.

CHUNK #3 — MIDDLE B: THE END OF THE MIDDLE

If you view a plot framework like an elaborate tug of war, the beginning is where the protagonists pick up the other end of the rope (the antagonists being the ones who arranged the match in the first place) and wonder what the hell the rope is for. They are nearly jerked off their feet at the beginning of the middle as the antagonists begin to pull. As the protagonists work it out, they begin to pull back around the middle of the story, but it is a setup: the antagonists were just measuring their strength, and at the end of the middle, they haul fiercely on the rope. The protags tumble forwards: they lose one man, but then the rest recoup in the beginning of the end, discover tensile strength they never knew they had, and work together to pull their furious antagonists forward into the mud pit. This chunk is the part where the antagonists get the upper hand.

Even that lame-ass little story has a bit of zing. At this stage of the editing process, you will want to check your manuscript for the ways in which it needs to conform to (or subvert) this classical piece of literary sorcery.

Second half of middle

The second half of the middle is typically a 'race against the clock' phase. A good amount of your action ought to be in this section. This is an extremely important part of the book, as it is either the place where your readers begin to speed up and get excited, or the place where a reader is most likely to put it down and not pick it back up again. What you're really wanting to do here is drive tension and conflict in the lead-up to the crisis at the end of the middle.

This part of a novel is often characterized by frustration. Under pressure from the sudden uptick in the stakes, tempers fray and your protagonist starts wondering whether they can pull it off. In a good Middle B chunk, they only win token victories that don't help them with the crisis, and are thwarted by themselves or others as they struggle on. They must abandon or revise their old goals and create new ones.

End of the middle

At the end of the middle, both the protagonists and antagonists have committed to their final goals: generally, the protagonists want to stop the antagonists from doing whatever they're doing, while the antagonists often want to achieve something unpleasant for the protagonists and possibly a lot of other people. If the end of the beginning is a commitment, the end of the middle is a rollercoaster plunge into Hell.

Even with the heightened stakes, all of your protagonist's efforts seem for naught. As the characters close in on their goal, you, the author, reach a point where you roll up your sleeves, grab a hammer, and start laying into your protagonist like a malevolent deity. The crisis is a point of acute pain: The hero's lover dies. The heroine's goal turns out to be a trap and the city is destroyed. The wizard loses control of his powers, or gets his powers stripped from him. The spaceship oxygen fails, leaving the team with only three hours of air before they turn into astronaut food. Something horrible, ecstatic, or otherwise compelling occurs here. Generally, it is found in the last chapters leading up to the end. You also generally resolve some subplots in this region of the story.

CHUNK #4 – THE END: CRISIS AND CLIMAX

You're on the home-stretch, now. Your characters got on that rollercoaster, they're in Hell, and now they have to kill the demon and find their way back before the portal closes.

The end is essentially your protagonists' reactions to the crisis at the end of the middle. They react to this crisis with a sense of finality. It's do or die from here on, and they are determined (or resigned) to participating. Your characters find what they need in themselves to follow through on the story goal – whatever it takes.

The end is often easy to write and difficult to edit. This is a good reason to look at the end early on in your editing process. The beginning is often the easiest to edit, so make sure to save some energy to fix the end of your book as well. Self-editors often leave a number of errors in the end section because they've obsessed so much over the beginning that they run out of puff.

The beginning of the end often requires some sort of meeting or convocation between characters. In the case of single protags, they often must go through a thought process or identity experience that mirrors the kind of decision-making process that a group would go through.

Climax

The climax is where all of your unresolved plotlines converge into an epic finale. Win or lose, this is crunch time. The important thing isn't whether the novel ends on a happy note or a tragic one, or anything in between, but whether or not it offers *catharsis*. More on that later.

The crisis near the end of a novel can be anything, but it is the tipping point that drives the action on to the climactic end scenes of the book. There is often a kind of re-commitment to the plot by the protagonist at this point. As an editor, what you are really looking for at this point is energy. Energy is quite possibly the last thing you are feeling by the time you've read to this point in your manuscript for the third time, but that dynamic, pumping energy is what you need to focus on at this stage of a story. The reader is invested in the characters and the outcome at this point, and so you, as the author, are completely entitled to screw with their emotions. Find your 'pain points', as they like to say in marketing, and twist them up to a barely comfortable level that you hold until the moment of relief... or the moment of ultimate horror, if you swing that way.

Denouement or lead-In

Following the climax, you can do one of two things (or somehow both at the same time, if you're clever): you can write what's called a denouement, otherwise known as a come down, which gives the reader some closure after the emotional rollercoaster of the book. Or, you can use this part to lead into the next part of the story (if the book is a series). George R.R Martin did a good job of this in *A Game of Thrones*, which ends with a very profound scene featuring Daenerys and her dead partner. By contrast, J.K Rowling screwed up for a lot of her fans with her series finale denouement. Be aware that if you impose firm decisions on your characters at this point, you're going to alienate some readers and please others. You have to balance your head and heart on that matter. If you're thinking ahead to your readers, you want the denouement to be satisfying, not trivializing. The worst examples of a denouement go something like: "And then the hero woke up!"

This part of the book is, in some ways, a gentler second catharsis. The climax was the emotional release, while the denouement is the 'aww!' moment, whether expressed with overtones of sympathy, pleasure, pride or grief. Funerals, weddings, ceremonies can and often do feature in these wrap-up scenes, cementing the 'new world' in a ritualized, affirming way.

If, for some reason, you can't find these peaks and valleys of your story, you may have a problem. Your story may be lacking in tension or have poor pacing if you can't break it down into energetic, dynamic sections. Even though all of these section locations are approximate, they exist in every good story, no matter what order they appear in.

ALTERNATIVES TO THE THREE-ACT STRUCTURE

The three acts and their various sections and components dominate English-language literature, but despite the impression given to most authors, it is not the only form of narrative structure in the world. The three-act structures I describe in this book were first articulated by Aristotle and then, many years later, by a German playwright named Gustav Freytag. *Fix Your Damn Book!* is very much aimed at American writers of genre fiction, and Freytag's Triangle – which could almost be referred to as the Hollywood Standard Narrative these days – is what a lot of authors in the US need for success. However, it's not the only narrative structure that exists. All cultures have their own forms of storytelling, a few of which I will briefly cover.

Qijue (Chinese) or *Kishotenketsu* (Japanese) describes a story structure which is commonly employed in East Asian narratives which tends to focus on the rhythm of events in a given scene. Each scene leads to a natural progression of slowly escalating tension and relief in a circular pattern. Stories tend to be slower to build overall, but the cycle creates suspense 'in the moment' throughout each scene. This narrative style is extremely good for creating tension throughout the course of mundane activities, and many classic East Asian works of literature and film (and those influenced by them, such as Quentin Tarantino) are renowned for this.

There are four parts to the *qijue* narrative framework:

1. *Introduction*: Introducing the argument or topic;

2. *Development*: Details and elaboration on the introduction;

3. *Twist/Climax*: A sudden shift in the focus of the story, which creates interest and a sense of mystery. The perspective or focus of the scene often changes here;

4. *Conclusion*: A wrap-up of the events inclusive of the twist.

A brief example of the structure would be something like: A girl goes into her favorite bakery to buy a meat pastry (introduction). The baker comments that the girl usually buys a custard bun, not anything with meat on it: the girl smiles, but says nothing (development). The scene cuts to the baker as he goes out behind his shop and finds the girl feeding the pastry to an alley cat (twist; note the change in focus from girl to baker). The girl explains that this cat has just had kittens, and points to a dumpster where kittens are meowing (conclusion).

Qijue is highly circular, and the structure is used at the micro and macro levels: it can be used to inform an entire story or a single paragraph.

The interesting thing about 'Conclusions' in *Qijue/Kishotenketsu* structures is that the ending is not necessarily the high point of the story – the 'twist' replaces the typical Greek theatre-inspired climax we are used to in Western literature and film, meaning that Japanese and Chinese films often 'peak' about three-quarters of the way through with a powerful revelation, and the ending can often be frustratingly inconclusive to Western audiences. This is why so many East Asian narratives end in death or leave-taking, rather than a seeming final triumph – the victory occurred earlier in the story! If you've ever watched an anime or read a manga that has an obtuse ending where everyone dies/disappears, you will know *exactly* what I'm talking about.

If you're heavily influenced by anime and manga, you probably use this structure unconsciously to some extent, so do your research and keep *kishotenketsu* in mind as you edit. Reading up on the structures of Japanese and Chinese theatre couldn't hurt, either, as *Jo-ha-kyu* (the Japanese theatrical dramatic arc) is quite relevant to books influenced by or set in Japan, China and Korea. One of the best accessible examples for English readers is *Journey to the West*, the story which was turned into the famous TV series *Monkey*.

Storytelling has been a huge part of African cultures for a very long time in many different forms, and contemporary African and Afro-American narrative structures still draw off many of the old storytelling forms that developed in various parts of Africa.

African narrative structures are essentially founded in an oral storytelling tradition, and the spoken word is the foundation of African literature. Instead of a 'three act' structure, African narratives are generally characterized by a 'call and response' where tension is driven by the interactions between people first and foremost. Small elements are played off one another in a gradually escalating fashion, forming a kind of narrative zig-zag pattern. Villains rarely exist in the way they're painted in European stories – even the worst person is generally driven by very human needs, compelled by something against their will (anything from witchcraft to the need for money or food), or they are mischievous and amoral. My observation is that African narratives tend to loop back around to the beginning in a fairly overt fashion, often following a very sudden and rapid climax. Modern African narratives – both on the continent and around the world – are now very heavily influenced by Hollywood. In America, there are many examples of African-American authors who blend the African oral storytelling methodology with Euro-Greek linear narrative to create works of fiction. *Beloved* by Toni Morrison comes straight to mind.

Eastern Europe has a distinctive narrative style which lends itself well to epic fantasy and other really long kinds of novels, a style which often splits stories into very defined acts which are each written as their own narrative arc. There is a basic 'Western' literary structure to Russian literature, but the Eastern European style tends to be slower to build than what is common in Hollywood-style storytelling. There are often expansive segues into the relationship between characters and their environment, with conflict between people often being expressed less by their interactions with each other, and more by their individual interactions with the world around them. This can lead to a 'wandering narrative' that doesn't often exist in English-language stories. Vassili might have a quest to go and find a golden sword, but nine-tenths of his story are devoted to his journey, which segues into confrontations with witches, assisting people in distress, and struggles in hostile environments. He will accomplish his quest almost as an afterthought.

One of the best current examples of this accessible to Anglo-English folks is *The Witcher* series of games and the novels written by Polish author Andrzej Sapowski. *The Witcher* is notable for the way it positions its hero, Geralt, as an actor-in-the-world, frequently drawn into seemingly tangential encounters which inevitably end with him coming out like a badass. Like many Slavic heroes, Geralt seems subject to the tides of the world around him, drawn into multiple wars despite his hatred of politics. He mopes about this a great deal (a common Eastern Bloc trope). A number of his stories have no satisfying ending, which is also something of a feature of Slavic literature.

There are many other narrative forms in the world, and this is a very superficial overview of the ones I personally know of. I am not inclined to try and generalize the story-telling traditions of Native America or Indigenous Australia – they had many narrative forms, languages, literary/oratory traditions and story-telling practices, and trying to sum them all up into a pithy paragraph on Indigenous narrative structure is detrimental to their efforts to reclaim their heritage as individual nations. If you are not Indigenous but are interested in the storytelling methods and narrative structures of an individual nation within your country, I suggest you contact them and have a chat with their elders about story.

In the current era, postmodernity has meant that many artists take inspiration from multiple cultural sources. I highly recommend that you contact writers and academics in different countries and communities to learn more about the different dramatic forms present in the world – and read widely, of course.

THE EDITOR'S TOOLBOX:

DEVELOPMENTAL EDITING

N ow that you have the structure of your book sorted and a good idea of what you need to rewrite, add, subtract or reconfigure within your plot, you can look at some of the smaller developmental elements that comprise your book.

The items in these toolbox sections are listed alphabetically, not in order of priority. Everyone's priorities, voice and story needs are different.

Accents, appearance, and culture

These three are treated together because they tend to relate.

We've all read fantasies where everyone has a British (or American) accent, or where the world is effectively a re-spun Middle Earth. Sadly, many novels feature a default pan-Anglo Saxon cast offset by tokenistic 'others' in nations based on stereotypes. This is beginning to change, but there are still problems.

When writing any character, you are going to have to depict both what makes them different from other characters in the story, and also what unifies them with the other characters, plot and setting. On the physical level, this is most frequently done through exposition on skin color, physical marks or features, accents and ways of speaking, and other similar details. When done skillfully, the world of the characters comes to life in a way that is engaging and authentic. When done poorly, everyone either sounds the same (erasing the unique voices and contributions of the cast) or fits into stereotypical race or species boxes.

Discussing real-world race and culture in fiction is nothing to fear, but requires a writer to avoid either stereotyping (through use of cheap tropes) or erasing (by mentioning nothing at all). The keys to this are communication with members of the communities you're writing about, and research.

One thing you often see are comparisons of people's skin tones to food. Using food similes to describe skin tone (her skin was as <color> as <food item>) might be effective, in that it is brief, but it is both objectifying and lazy. My challenge to you is to find other ways of describing people, gradually working details into the narrative instead of pointing out that someone is toffee, cream, spaghetti or coffee-colored. One other thing to look for is cliché description by exposition. A lot of people introduce their characters through a rote set of features in their early drafts. "She had wavy golden locks and blazing sapphire orbs beneath a scrunched up brow, an upturned nose and cupid's bow lips." Ick. Work the details in over time. Tease the reader with someone's appearance, and build their interest and regard for that person.

Accents, pitch and tone of voice are one way you can convey character. You have a few options on how to do this: you can write the accent, you can hint at the accent in dialogue, but not develop it beyond a word drop now and then, and/or you can note what accent the character has and not depict it. This is one of those really subjective 'voice' issues that varies from writer to writer.

If you want to know what different accents in English sound like, here is a useful online resource for listening to and understanding them: http://accent.gmu.edu/

Culture is the depth of 'place' behind any character. Poorly expressed culture tends to come out in exposition by dialogue. There are occasions where someone might say something like: "Sorry, I'm not used to people doing things like that." But unless they are somehow both close to the other characters in the story while also paradoxically being unfamiliar to them, you're never going to have some basic 'this is how we do things back home' conversation.

Our culture is expressed in the way that we relate to the world and people (and animals) around us. Body language, dress, modesty (or lack of it), family relationships (or lack of them), independence or codependence or communal dependence, and, of course, the way we relate to and treat people from other cultures. The vast majority of people are not interested in or capable of lecturing the naïve about 'their culture'. They simply demonstrate its traits. This is just as true of fantasy cultures as it is of Earth cultures.

Richter, one of the characters in my fantasy novel, was raised by multiple fathers – polyandry is typical in his culture. Older men are, by extension, regarded as the primary parental caregivers of his community. Why? War isn't on their radar, but protecting children from disease, cold and hunger is. There is barely any arable land to farm in his homeland, so while the women weave, plant and trade, the men herd with their children on their backs and give them milk from the animals they rear. Concepts common to other places in the world: parents leaving children to be raised by surrogates, mothers rearing multiple children alone while the father works, gender segregation in matters of decision making, wet-nurses living at a home so that a woman doesn't have to nurse her own child – these things are foreign to a man from the Tuun.

Having him sit down to explain this like a storybook lesson to his compatriots, even if was relevant to the story, would be a bit cringeworthy. Instead, it is better to work these parts of Richter's history into his current actions. For example, he may be hesitant to accept only a single opinion from an authority figure in a foreign country where royalty considers themselves inherently 'better' than commoners. One person making the rules doesn't feel 'right', even if Richter knows, intellectually, that's how things work in Ilia. He may naturally assume a fatherly attitude to younger people, because that's what he grew up with: communal parentage is a duty for men in the Tuun, with decisions made by campfire consensus. He may express initial confusion at the significance of bastardry in feudal cultures, followed by privately held disdain. These are some of the more obvious ways that this character's background could be worked into the narrative over time. It's useful for suspense and conflict, too – culture often affects the way we make decisions, and the standards we make those decisions by. The way something pans out in the story might make one character happy, and leave the other uncomfortable.

Other, smaller things include the way that a character counts (does every place use the same numeric system? Every country, every planet?), the way they use their hands (if they do use a ten-digit numeric system, do children count from their thumb or from their pinkie?), the way they use their eyes (is meeting the eyes of another person respectful or not? Friendly or not?), the peculiar cadence of the voice (for example, some languages don't 'lift' the last word of a sentence when asking a question: they use a question 'word' or particle, or rely on the context of the sentence.) There's any number of ways to express appearance, background and locality without resorting to food-based skin tones, exaggerated accents, or superficial 'othering'.

Another feature to consider about culture is that it is generally shaped by the local environment. Italians living in Rome and Italians living in Australia have very different cultures, even if they fundamentally identify as 'Italian'. Chinese expats living in Italy have a different culture again, as do Mongolians living in Russian cities vs those living on the Steppe vs those living in Hong Kong. Elves living in cities and elves who grew up in the forest won't have the same culture – and neither will elves who grew up in different cities and different forests from one another. If your setting is mountainous and difficult to transverse, consider how many languages might have evolved in those inaccessible valleys?

Confused? Don't be. Rendering culture is a complex task, but it's also really fun. As above, the key is to do your research and contact representatives of the communities you're writing about (or who embody traits you want to represent in a fictional culture). Info-dumps, however, are not your friend. Find ways to edit them into something more dynamic.

Balancing description, exposition and action

People generally go one of two ways when they first sit down with their manuscript. Either they start adding in material until the manuscript bloats, or they strip the meat from it in their desperation and turn their work into a skeleton of its former self. As it so often is, the key is balance. You have to know what to strip and what to leave.

Description and exposition are both used to explain stuff in the environment or setting, or about the characters. Description is mostly *showing* – you're painting a picture of something with words. It can be detailed or suggestive or somewhere in between, depending on the requirements of the scene. Exposition is where you're *telling* the reader something. Because this is a form of telling rather than showing, exposition needs to be very relevant, easy and fast to read.

Both description and exposition are necessary to tell a story, but they're also risky to dwell upon. They interrupt your pacing if they're not immediately relevant to what's happening in the scene. Early in a book, when readers are not yet heavily invested in the end, too much showing OR telling can be what causes them to put your book down and not pick it up again.

That doesn't mean you shouldn't describe a place or person or omit important information. You need some description in your work: otherwise, everything is just an empty room. Too much description, and it becomes a chore that people skim over. Too little exposition, and the reader has no context: too much exposition, and the reader is being spoonfed the details in your world which they long to investigate, imagine, and solve themselves.

Let's say you're writing a science fiction story, and your story has a really cool spaceship that the Protag and her crew fly around in. It has a propulsion system that is based on hard science and is a real possibility in the future, and it has a sentient computer and is beautiful and functional and has a huge graceful-looking console with silver and gold trim and... great. I assure that next to no one will care about the gold trim until after they are invested in the computer's personality, and the people and aliens who use the ship as transport. In the beginning, you typically have to break this stuff up into smaller pieces. Shorter sentences have to carry more of your description and exposition. The further you go into the book, the more of these two things you can do – but not in the beginning, and definitely not on the first three pages. If you have to, give hints by setting your characters up in an evocative place and scenario. There's a zombie war coming, and the protagonist hears it on the radio and goes to buy bottled water at Walmart and gets into a gun fight with already-desperate, paranoid people. You don't have to lay out the history of how zombies came to be, how far the zombies are from the Walmart, and what the Walmart looks like. It's all about the emotional value of seeing people do things.

Even books later in a series should avoid doing this at all possible. Recaps are tempting and sometimes necessary, but whether you're writing the first book or the eleventh in a series, try to open with some kind of dynamic event instead of a static revision of previous books.

Avoiding dry description is vital in the context of your opening line and paragraph. A prison guard calling for order. A radio announcer talking about war. Those are both people doing things. The solution to bloating and skinning is to focus your descriptions and expositions in the moment. This means that you demonstrate what is happening instead of describing it:

(Dry) Description: 'The Warden – a huge, cybernetically enhanced juggernaut of muscle and bio-steel – was furious, and he was getting close to Ricardo's cell to break up the fight'.

Exposition: *'Ricardo had been imprisoned for aggravated assault, even though he hadn't committed the crime. He was anxiously awaiting the Warden, who was constantly on edge from the hundred needling indignities he faced every day as the head of Corrective Services on the Carthage, the largest prison ship in the Andromeda Quadrant.'*

Demonstration: *'Ricardo stared at his hands as the Warden's heavy bootstep echoed down the hall. The screaming and fighting outside his cell had stopped. Nothing broke up a fight faster than the crack of metal on metal, the Warden's truncheon striking metal with inhuman strength as he drew it across the bars on the* *way upstairs.*

"You little bastards feel like taking a trip out the airlock or what?" The Warden's deep voice boomed down the echoing cargo-ship corridor. Voices always seemed louder in space. "Shut the fuck up, all of you!"

Showing actually involves some 'telling' (especially in third-person), which confuses a lot of people. Your challenge is to avoid something we call 'narrative imposition' in Editorland. Narrative imposition is what happens in the first and second example paragraphs above. You, the author, is explaining what is happening in a given scene. When you verge into explanation, it throws the reader out of the story, and frequently results in boredom.

There is a threshold level of explanation involved in showing/demonstrating. 'Ricardo stared at his hands' is still you telling the reader what is going on, but in such a way as to be unobtrusive. This is the technical reasoning behind the common advice to authors about avoiding adverbs: good narrative deemphasizes the narrator's explanations.

'Fred said' is the narrator tagging who has spoken in a piece of dialogue, but it is effectively invisible. We will know the context by Fred's other actions: his smile, his hands on his hips, his sly expression or his laughter. By contrast, 'Fred said jokingly' imposes a condition on the 'saying', directing the reader to think or feel a certain way that they may not *actually be feeling*. What if they thought Fred said it half-heartedly, or sarcastically? The narrator is imposing their view on something which is better left to the imagination of the reader.

If you can read something aloud and it sounds a bit

like a god pointing their finger at the scene and describing it, you're imposing on your own story. 'Ricardo was frightened' won't cut it. Ricardo isn't actually *doing* anything when you say that. The narrator is telling us that he is feeling a particular way because the narrator is lazy. Find a way to show it from Ricardo's level of existence: His mouth is dry and his hands are sweaty. Trust the reader to figure it out from there.

Once upon a time...

There is one significant exception to the above advice: fairytales and narratives which seek to emulate the classic structure of fables and fairytales. These stories often open with a narrator's voice which is used to frame the story – 'Once upon a time' is the most well-known introduction to this kind of story. There is often an element of narrator imposition in fairytales, along with a decent amount of exposition to establish concrete images which must be conveyed a certain way. But this doesn't mean your story should be bloated with exposition. This technique is called 'Narrative Framing' and should be used judiciously and only within certain kinds of story.

Mysteries are another genre which often requires some narrative framing, which is one of the reasons that so many mystery, crime and detective novels are written in first-person. The point-of-view exposition of the investigator can lead to interesting red herrings, mistakes, breakthroughs, or half-remembered clues.

The world around us

When it comes to describing scenery, less is usually more. This can, ironically, be done by fixating on the details of the scene you're trying to set. 'A cornfield in Kansas at sunset' evokes a static image, but the hazy red sky, the clouds blazing in lines towards the horizon, and the cooling wind whispering over dry corn stalks are details which can draw someone into the memory of a place they have never seen.

There are some very notable exceptions to the less-is-more thing: those authors who are, at heart, worldbuilders. Clive Barker, Frank Herbert, Terry Pratchett, Tolkien and China Miéville are all authors who lavish on their settings, pausing their stories to elaborate on the world and setting itself. How did they get away with this, in light of the above? Easy: they turn their worlds into characters in their own right, and they use those pauses to create suspense by leaving the outcome of the preceding action in a state of uncertainty. In addition, they often have a masterful command of the language, and they write exposition for the sheer beauty of the words:

"I rinsed linen in the pond, I stared at the brewhouse. Like all these long low squat houses, it had been not for but against. They were built against the forest, against the sea, against the elements, against the world... as though in this part of the world an architect always included hatred among his tools, and said to his apprentice: "Mind you've bought along enough hatred today." Jane Gaskell, Some Summer Lands.

All of those authors are either fantasy authors, literary fiction authors, or both. If your voice and story really needs that kind of expository world-building, then make sure that your setting has the personality and weight of a central character. Then you'll know what to do.

Catharsis

Catharsis literally means 'purification' or 'cleansing'. Along with characters, catharsis is probably one of the core reasons that we read and write fiction.

Catharsis was first articulated as a concept in Ancient Greece, where it was used by Aristotle to describe the emotional effects of tragedy on the audience at the theater. A cathartic incident causes a great swelling of emotion, followed by mingled feelings of emptiness and longing, gratification and relief. It's basically how your readers (and you!) get so wrapped up in your story that the character's suffering becomes their suffering, and the purge of that suffering – which happens through the victory or heroic failure of the characters – becomes their purging.

Cathartic scenes have a powerful effect on the reader. The end of *The Lord of the Rings* trilogy has an archetypal cathartic moment, where Frodo literally hurls his burden (the ring) into a volcano and then has to escape the climactic explosion. To borrow a cinematic example, the animated film *Ghost in The Shell* has a powerful cathartic moment: the point where Kusanagi, straining to open the entry to the walking tank trying to kill her, literally tears herself apart with effort and falls limply to the ground. It is a moment of ultimate pathos, which is shortly followed by a scene of ultimate transcendence. And that transcendence – the moment where your hero is demonstrably more-than-human – is the key to good catharsis in fiction.

The essence of your catharsis may not be as dramatic as those examples, but you can still engage the cathartic switch by contrasting tragedy (or, arguably, any powerful emotional experience) and transcendence. Even a non-fantasy protagonist or antagonist can have these moments. Good thrillers are full of them (Clarice's terror and victory in *Silence of the Lambs*; Silas' last stand in *The DaVinci Code*). Mysteries are full of them (Sherlock Holme's plunge off a cliff with Moriarty), and so is literary fiction (*Beloved*) and Magical Realism (*Hard Boiled Wonderland at the End of the World* by Haruki Murakami, amongst many others). Hollywood is very aware of the power of catharsis. If you've ever wondered how movies like *Avatar* – aka. *Blue Pocahontas Dances with Wolves in Fern Gully* – become so popular, it's because they offer catharsis. There's a reason the Death Star explodes instead of just shutting down and turning dark.

As you're reading through, note the cathartic moments in your novel – or the absence of them. If you feel like anything is missing a bit of 'spark', cathartic situations are what might be missing. Label these incidents or absences when you find them and see what you can do to invoke a sense of wonder and relief.

Characters

You could argue that characters are the reason we write and/or read novels at all. They are the actors in your story, and to write realistic characters, you need to observe real people who approximate your characters doing things. Research, research, research. Watching videos is effective, as is observing them in person.

To get your characters doing what you want them to, you may find it helpful to write a short (one sentence; two at most) character story arc for each character in your plot planner. If you discover you have characters without a strong story arc, merge them into other characters. The same applies for walk-in characters who have nothing significant to do with the story and who don't serve any practical function. Just because they're funny and interesting doesn't make them necessary. Merge their funny dialogue into more significant characters where appropriate.

Another mistake that is easy to correct: if you have lots of characters, try giving them names beginning with different letters of the alphabet. This helps the reader (and you) keep the names in order as they read. Editors in publishing houses recommend this because it helps a reader keep track of all the characters. If you have multiple characters with names that begin with 'H', consider keeping the best name and change the others.

You can reliably omit or transform any scenes where a character is doing something and thinking. Brushing their hair and thinking. Looking in a mirror and thinking. Perching on skyscrapers in the darkness and thinking. This works best in film, but not so well in prose. Turn their thoughts into a conversation or activity when possible. Greetings, daily routines (unless particularly unusual, and then you only need to mention them once) and other mundane activities are rarely required in novels.

Establishing strong characterization in the beginning of your novel is very difficult, no doubt about it. As an editor, you are looking for three things at this stage: a clear visual (preferably created without excessive description), a sense of personality, and action/activities which characterize the character. It is unwise to have more than one or two significant characters in your opening pages.

- When we first meet your character, what are they doing? Is it something that embodies them, whether through duty, profession, identity, culture or passion? Dexter is a serial killer, so what do you think he's doing at the beginning of *Darkly Dreaming Dexter*?

- Long-winded descriptions of physical traits – hair, eyes, skin, etc. – should be challenged and either omitted (either in their entirety, or included in smaller pieces later on in the story) or shortened. Descriptions of psychological traits (Lady Kieran was a shy princess) should be universally purged, unless one character is describing another. Instead of describing the character, focus on painting them through their actions. If you character is tall and athletic, show them running and having to duck a door instead of telling us that they have a tall, athletic build. Brief descriptions can work if you need to have them, but should definitely be avoided for the MC at this stage.

- Do your characters have individual patterns of speech? Read the first line of dialogue each one of your characters speak aloud, and see if the people sound the same. If they do, fix it. It's even worse is if they all sound like you.

- Would you hear people talking like your characters in the street? If someone said your character's lines to you in real life, what would you think of how they sounded?

- If you've used adverbs to characterize characters, pick the adverb out into a demonstration of that character's nature. I see this most often with the words 'sarcastically' and 'whining', because demonstrating sarcasm and cowardice requires more effort as a writer than, say, demonstrating niceness or toughness.

One of the harder questions to ask about your characters is: "Are they interesting?" The definition of 'interesting' is going to vary from author to author, but if you find that one or other of your characters seems to fall a bit flat, work in some background and color to their lives.

Head-hopping and faulty exposition

If you're the kind of author who switches character points of view within paragraphs, you have an awful lot of work to do. Yes, some books have gotten through the gate with POV switching in the same paragraph or chapter – *Dune* comes to mind – but the style is somewhat outdated as of the 2010's. Multiple point-of-view switches within scenes or chapters is generally now only done by authors with some experience and contacts in the industry. Newbies will not get away with it in their debut.

The main reason this technique has fallen out of favor is that it confuses the reader, and the reader is not the person you want to confuse. It also makes it harder to develop significant empathic rapport with the experiences of a particular character if they are always chopping and changing around. Just like when you use short adverbial phrases to tell people things, head-hopping is a lazy way of trying to show the reader everything in a scene. If your story has multiple POV sections, you will need to find some way to cleanly and efficiently delineate them. New chapters are best, ala *A Game of Thrones*. Asterisks and spaces between paragraphs will do in a pinch, if you're determined to switch characters within a single chapter.

There are plenty of ways to get insight into multiple characters within a single scene. You can reveal their minds through dialogue, action, brief exposition, and your head-character's perspective on the activity around them. Arguments can be good ways for characters to exchange information without switching to 'he thought and then she thought'.

One pernicious POV error is the description of a character's actions, thoughts or perceptions *while in the head of a particular character*. For example: "I wracked my brains while massaging my skull with a meaty, well-worn hand." The first part of this sentence, "I wracked my brains…" is something I call 'narrative distance', which we discuss more in the line editing section. The 'massaging my skull with a meaty, well-worn hand' bit is the main point-of-view error.

How do you know? Well, when you're rubbing your face, do you generally note that your hand is anything other than your hand? Do you say it aloud? My guess is that you just rub your damn face or massage your scalp and not really pay attention to whether your hand is meaty or not. You may, at some point, contemplate your hands for some reason, at which point you may note their relative meatiness or lack thereof. But in the moment? No. That's the God-like narrator pointing their finger at the character and screaming: "LOOK! HE HAS THICK HANDS! LOOK AT ME SENPAI!"

Does this sound awfully like narrative imposition? That's because it is. It's specifically a form of narrative imposition that is common (and very, *very* occasionally necessary to establish context) in first-person POV.

Another example would be where the POV character looks at a computer screen and the light gleams off the outside of their glasses or eyes in the description. As a glasses-wearer who spends a lot of time in front of a computer, I can assure you that I cannot see my own eyes from the perspective of the monitor. Now, if the POV character is *watching* Hacker McBrainyson at the desktop and the light is reflecting off *their* glasses, then your protagonist may notice this depending on how observant and detail-orientated they are. However, it might be more in-character for them to be looking at the hentai posters on his wall, or the betta swimming in a bowl next to his bed. Write what the character is most likely to see.

Lazy writing

Can you find the lazy writing in your draft? Everyone cuts corners while they're drafting, the better to get their ideas onto paper. There's a few giveaways.

Firstly, adverbs, adverbs, adverbs. Adverbs often indicate areas where you're cheesing out. Any time you spot those cheeky '-ly' words, have a think about whether or not you were skipping over in that scene. If you have a compacted activity where speed is not a factor, then try to unpick it a bit and see how it flows.

Dreams, fast-forwards/time-skips, hallucinations, sleep and unconsciousness also often indicate areas of laziness, unless they're really relevant to the plot. These can often be removed if they're related to transitional periods and you're trying to speed a journey.

Laziness is often found where there are drops in tension or suspense. This isn't the same as, for example, cutting out the 'Hello?' and 'It's me' transactions on a phone call. Laziness that decreases suspense are things like the old: "And then he woke up!" or the appearance of a blatant Deus Ex Machina, a god-like presence who descends from on high with the express purpose of bringing a scene or story to a close and who is never seen again.

Plot holes

Plot holes occur when a plot or sub-plot conflicts with other plotlines, and either doesn't resolve or resolves in a way that contradicts the other parts of the story. This is what your plot planner is for, and it is a very good reason to use different colors to delineate different plots and sub-plots. You have braided the story together during the writing phase, but editing requires you to unweave that braid and examine the strands for compatibility. If a sub-plot doesn't work, cut it out of the book and save it in a separate file – you might be able to use it for future works.

Point-of-view: first, second, and third-person perspectives

This stage of editing is where you really need to lock in your perspective. There's four basic point-of-view perspectives in English: eye of the beholder (first-person), conversational (second-person), observer from the inside (third-person intimate) and eye of god (third-person omniscient).

- First-person is as if you, the narrator, were the

protagonist: the story uses 'I' and 'we' or variants thereof to refer to themselves, and observes other characters and settings from this perspective. The author essentially takes the role of the main POV character/s. The most intimate form of narration. Example: Jim Butcher's *The Dresden Files.*

- Second-person is as if you were having a conversation with the reader, and *they* are the protagonist. It's the kind of narration a dungeon master uses to direct a character around a dungeon. "You enter the limousine where the Senator is waiting." Example: R.L Stein's *Goosebumps 'Choose Your Own Adventure'* books.

- Third-person intimate is where you write from an external perspective (out of the character's head), but follow the thoughts, gesture and observational field of only *one* character. This is currently the most popular perspective in modern genre fiction, closely followed by first-person. The trick is to imagine a camera on your character's shoulder which moves as they do, recording only what they can see, but not from behind their own eyes. Example: J.K Rowling's *Harry Potter* series.

- Third-person omniscient is where you narrate as if you were an eye in the sky, capable of seeing, hearing and depicting everything that occurs in the narrative, including the thoughts or activities of multiple characters. This was a very popular perspective in early science-fiction. Example: Frank Herbert's *Dune.*

As you might expect, the line between the different 'distances' possible with third-person is often blurry. Stories can and do expand into omniscient when outlaying a scene or setting and then narrow the focus back to the POV character. If you write in third-person, check over to make sure that the widening of your narrative field is controlled, rather than see-sawing between intimate and omniscient at random.

There is no one perspective that is better than any other, though certain perspectives suit particular genres more readily than others. As mentioned, third-person intimate is currently the most popular, perhaps because it mimics the film or television experience and gives the reader a deep understanding of a single person. Your choice of perspective very much depends on your style, voice and genre. Romance, being an intimate genre, benefits from intimate perspectives. Science-fiction and epic fantasy are often less focused on the intimate lives of the characters, and third-person omniscient is more common in these genres. That's not to say that you can't or shouldn't use a given point-of-view for any particular story, but if you're determined to write yourself a third-person omniscient romance with a cast of thousands, you've certainly set yourself an interesting challenge.

If you have written your novel in second-person, I sure hope it's an experimental literary work and not something you want to sell well in a genre market. It is an extremely difficult perspective to do well for long periods of time, as readers quickly become frustrated when they are told what to do over the course of a story. One of the best authors to use second-person POV was Franz Kafka, so if you're wanting to dabble, I recommend you read his short stories.

Generally speaking, you pick one perspective and stick to it throughout the novel. Some books successfully play with perspective, swapping it around and changing between chapters. This is more common in literary fiction than it is in genre fiction, which conventionally employs one perspective throughout the entire novel. In that case, check your manuscript for strategic consistency – it doesn't have to be 'typical', but it does have to be congruent!

Pacing

Pacing is a huge factor in any book. Many first-time authors are so eager to get into the action (because that's what we are told we should do, and often) that they cram too much into the first page at the expense of suspense. Your first page shouldn't be like one of those horrible old Tripod-hosted websites, crammed with flashing .gif files and obnoxious midi tunes. At this crucial early stage, your reader doesn't know any of your characters. If there's nothing to break up your dialogue and actions, they get no sense of who these people are and why they should care about them.

- Do you have stand-alone dialogue without associated actions to break up people speaking? Add actions.

- Is all dialogue and every action clearly assigned? Make sure they are.

- Are there indications of body-language, mannerisms, tone, mood? Add them in.

- Could the actions of your first pages be transferred to any setting without significant changes made? If so, it isn't well grounded in the setting you intended. If your city-skyline fight could be moved to an open desert with only the addition of sunlight or sand, you will need to rewrite it to better place it within the intended setting: the dizziness of inertia at a great height, the swaying of the skyscraper underfoot.

- In addition, do you notice that this opening scene could be done by any character, not just your MC? Stepping out of a car is a good example. Anyone can step out of a car onto a crime scene. What is something only YOUR character could do?

Screen for slow-moving scenes, sentences, or for 'participial phrases'. These are sentences which typically begin with an '-ing' word: 'Having moved from the table, the Queen picked up her letter from the Herald's tray and anxiously toyed with it in her fingers.'

Unless you're really in love with this as a stylistic thing, rewrite these sentences into an active voice. You will often do well to break participial phrases into two sentences.

A good rule of thumb is that each sentence should do one thing or carry through one action at a time. "With a sigh, the Queen moved from the table. She picked up the letter, turned it over, set it down again on the tray. "Thank you, goodman. But please just... leave it by the door."

Also, telling the reader about your world through dialogue between characters – also called exposition through dialogue – is a really bad way to hide clumsy exposition:

"Nazis? What are those?" Fred gasped.

"Well, after the fire at the Reichstag in 1933..." George explained.

I see what you did there. Agents and editors reviewing your manuscript know to look for this kind of thing, too. Beware.

Scenes

A scene is a block of action in your manuscript that progresses the plot. This is a very specific definition. Progresses the plot. No matter how you choose to structure your book, every single scene MUST push the plot (or sub-plots) forward in some way.

Now that we have a definition of suspense, you can probably make the connection that scenes are, ideally, either creating suspense or resolving suspense at any given time. The rhythm of this build and release of tension is a unique part of your voice, and will depend entirely on your tastes and the requirements of your genre.

You might have one scene per chapter or several scenes per chapter. In all instances, you must ask yourself:

- Does the scene belong in the book? Does it advance the action and enrich the story?
- If a scene is between two or more characters, does it advance the story or character development arc between those characters? This includes all sex scenes and romantic or witty bromantic/sismantic interludes.
- Do you give the characters time to reflect, plan, and make decisions? This is not the same as a 'filler' scene where someone is doing something prosaic, like going to the bathroom because

they need to. Some of the best character development comes out of scenes where characters are fielding ideas or engaged in suspenseful planning. These 'downtime' scenes often end with an explosive revelation, or a new problem which is encountered during the time of reflection.

Every scene has a beginning, middle and end of its own, from the opening line through to the conclusion of the scene and the beginning of the next. It should have a small conflict of its own, too: either internal, interpersonal, or external. But remember the previous warnings about 'slice of life' material, characters staring into mirrors, characters thinking while eating their Cheerios, etc.

Let's say that your Protag and her love interest are involved in a key scene where they are breaking into EvilCorp's headquarters. The two ladies stealth into the lobby and the conclusion of the scene is that they look up, see a camera pointed at them, and gas begins to fill the room. Before we reach that mini-climax, the scene still has to have suspense of some kind played throughout. This could be the whispered banter that distracts them from the presence of the camera. Maybe they thought to take out all the other cameras by cutting the power, but this particular one runs on an independent power source and they weren't expecting it to be running. Maybe they ninja in over and through lasers and get through, only to cop a face full of gas anyway. You get the gist. A scene where they just waltz into the museum and nothing challenges them until "SUDDENLY, DOOM!" is blah, at best.

Novelist and writing instructor Holly Lisle, in her book *How to Plan Your Story Revision*, puts it very well when she says: "End the scene at the point where the conflict is either made worse, or [is] resolved in some fashion. Cut any material that goes on after this point – save it to insert in a later scene if it's truly important."

You should jot down all scenes you plan to keep on your plot planner, as well as note all of the scenes you've cut. If you've removed reference to something at an early stage, make sure it's gone at a later stage. I generally use a numeric system which keeps track of scenes by chapter. My novel *Blood Hound,* for example:

Chapter 1 – Saturday 10th July, 1991 (around 11pm)

> 1.1 – Alexi deals with Moni in the car. Moni is being annoying while Alexi is trying to mentally prepare for the hit on Semyon. Scene goals: establish Alexi as a mage and as an intelligent, thoughtful, unusually contemplative person for his role (hitman).
>
> *1.2* – The car stops and Alexi and Moni receive their final instructions. Moni is thuggish and disgusting; we see Alexi's displeasure at having to work with him. *Add more conflict between them; interaction is bland at this stage.*
>
> 1.3 – Alexi and Moni enter Semyon's apartment and defuse a magical trap in the stairwell (created by J on assignment, later reveal). Scene reveals the scope of Alexi's magical ability and the Wardbreaker.
>
> And so on.

Also, as you work through scenes, it's important to

keep track of time and place. You must make certain that your characters are feasibly able to get from place to place in the time you've given them. As an action novel, *Blood Hound* is set within a very short time-frame – all of the events are crammed into a week and a half – and so keeping track of the time of day is important. Your timeframe may be longer or shorter depending on what you're writing, and time of day may be incidental rather than crucial.

The Ripple Effect

Changes you make near the beginning of your manuscript will have a ripple effect on the rest of the book. As you become more familiar with the structure of your manuscript, you will start to really get a sense of how the story is put together and what it needs to function properly, but it is easy to end up with plot holes and 'dead end' subplots: plots that you used to have in the book which are partially cut out of the manuscript as you revise it, but that now end suddenly and don't resolve.

To smooth this out – and to keep track of any changes you make – nothing beats index cards. Use them to mark your plot and the changes you have made to it at various points in the editing process. Authors and screenwriters have used index cards or index card-like things since time immemorial because they work, and they work *really* well. Whether you use a program like Scrivener or a pack of paper cards pinned on a corkboard, you can use cards to prevent and discover incongruities in your plot at this point of editing.

LINE EDITING

Brave writer, you boldly set off on your adventure. You crept through the gloomy forests of diagnosis, and battled until you were weary through the bloody fields of developmental editing. Welcome to the desert of line editing. I hope you bought a camel and lots of coffee.

By the time you start line editing, you should be pretty happy with your book as a whole. If you're not, then you should rest it again for a week or so, change the manuscript font, and go through developmental editing a second time with a re-drawn plot planner and your ideal synopsis. Then, come back and start your line editing.

If developmental editing is looking at macro issues of structure and pace, line editing is the examination of these things at a micro level. Previously, you snapped your manuscript down into chunks; now you're going to break it down into chapters, scenes, and paragraphs. You may also want break down into tears – the thought of picking over your book paragraph by paragraph is a bit much for gentle hearts. I recommend holding off on the breakdown until the copy editing stage. Syntax is all fun and games until the crying starts.

Seriously, though: developmental editing was the hardest stage, and if you're here, you're over the hump. Line editing is faster once you've got a few technical concepts down, and the foundation of your future labors are what I call the Three Cs.

THE THREE CS OF WRITING AND EDITING

The Three C's are *Congruency*, *Conflict*, and *Cadence*. We've touched on the first two already. Let's break them down for easy reference.

Congruency – Do all parts of the story agree with each other and make sense? Are your sentences correct and mean what you want them to mean? Does the story have gaps and plot holes, weak characters, or saggy middles? Is the story whole and believable?

Conflict – Are all scenes and interactions held under some kind of tension, obvious or covert? Are there catalytic moments of transformation? Why are you telling us *this* story in particular?

Cadence –Do the words in your manuscript – as you have assembled them – sound pleasing? Are they easily understandable when you read them aloud? Do you make use of tone, emotional rhythm, pace and word choice to style the effects you want in your work? Cadence is perhaps the most important of the three at the micro scale.

Creativity or *Character* could probably be added as the forth C, especially if you are using a *qijue*-style narrative structure and conflict doesn't feature as heavily. However, in the average English-language novel, these three factors are the lynchpins of good writing.

CONGRUENCY AT THE MICRO-SCALE

We discussed congruency as a part of developmental editing, but line editing is where you are really going to get cracking on it. You want to be looking for the little details now, examining each chapter, scene and paragraph to make sure they make sense and say the things you want them to say.

Congruency (pronounced 'con-gru-ency') is fundamentally related to 'making sense'. A story that isn't congruent is long-winded, frustrating, and ultimately unsatisfying. Congruency is doubly important for non-linear narratives and books intended to be part of a series – and if you're working on a series, the overall congruency of the series should *also* be in your mind while you edit your current manuscript.

What does your manuscript need to have it make sense? The biggest one is ensuring that all plotlines have a conclusion of some kind, even if the conclusion happens to be 'we don't know'. The characters (and the reader) can make peace with the mystery. What the reader won't make peace with is a plotline that just vanishes into thin air, no resolution given.

As we zoom down into semantics (meaning) and

syntax (the composition of words in sentences), congruency can mean making sure that your sentences are easy to understand. "Moreover, he forthwith endeavored to doff his coif," is not a particularly enjoyable sentence to try and interpret when: "He removed his hat and placed it against his chest," would work just as well.

A large part of congruency is making sure that your sentences are grammatical (in the sense that they mostly follow the rules of language) and that they have the correct register. Register refers to the style in which something is written. I recently put down a fairly well-known Indie novel within a few pages of picking it up. The book is marketed as urban fantasy/noir, but the register was off and it made my nose wrinkle. The following sentence was where I cringed and couldn't go back: "A faint pulse pushed back against my brawny digits."

Try reading that aloud and see where your tongue trips up. That kind of language might work in some fantasy or comedy novels (if you're into the cheese), but when I pick up an urban fantasy or noir story, I expect a certain kind of register. Dark, slick, the sentences pared down to an edgy hard-boiled quality. "I checked her pulse. It was light, quick, but it was there."

So congruency also means *tone.* Have you ever read a book that seemed to have a good concept, but the writing just didn't hit the spot for you? The tone was probably off. The problem that most writers face in the editing phase isn't that their tone is the wrong register for their story, but that they don't have a definite register at all. Their tone wanders from hard-boiled to whimsical, to middle-of-the-range nothingness, and then to some weird Olde English formality. Masterful writers will take a single register and apply it to stories that are familiar, and stories that don't usually use that register (a hard-boiled romance? Gritty fantasy? Lyrical horror?) and succeed just as well at both. Their secret is that they picked a tone, a style, and stuck with it. Jim Butcher, Patricia Briggs, Laurel K Hamilton, Neil Gaiman, China Mieville and Patrick Rothfuss are masters of this skill in different ways. You might not like one or any of these individual authors, but that's because you're not their audience. Their voice and command of tone and register is their brand, and their target markets eat it up.

How do you learn the patterns and use of language that defines a register? Study. Read books in your genre, watch films in your genre, and observe the common threads of language that link them, and practice.

If you're one of those people whose tone wanders around through the course of the manuscript, take a key scene from your book, open some blank documents, and try writing it in a specific tone. Try out a lyrical style, a formal style, a dark style, a hard-boiled style. See what fits best. Register is a tool you can learn to use.

In addition:

- Make sure that your chapters are in the right order for the course of the story. Are there any that stick out or that don't quite feel right as you read through them? You're probably correct. Trust your intuition and figure out where they should be.
- Are your scenes *contiguous*? Something that is contiguous forms an orderly, understandable

sequence. Do your scenes 'hook' into each other to create a proper flow of events?

- Does your opening line and opening scene bear any relation to the rest of the novel? This is actually a very common problem, especially in first novels. The events of the first scene should have some relevance to scenes later on in the book. If your first scene is orphaned from the rest of the story, think about how you can properly connect it to one of the major plot-threads.

- Are your paragraphs separated at the correct places? 'The correct places' generally occur when an environment changes, or someone's action ends and another person's action begins. This includes dialogue, so be sure to separate lines of dialogue into new paragraphs. Yes, even if they're only one word. Every time someone finishes speaking and emoting, hit 'Enter'.

- Are your sentences constructed the way you want them? Are they grammatically correct (applicable most of the time) or purposefully stylized but not necessarily grammatical (some of the time)?

- One useful little nibblet for line editing that I use for my own manuscripts: I tend to title each chapter 'Chapter One, Chapter Two' and so on during the draft phase, and once I reach the line editing phase, I change the numbers to numerals. As each chapter becomes 'Chapter 1, Chapter 2', I can keep track of where I am in the book just a little more easily. Plus, I get the sense that I am progressing through the work.

STRENGTHENING CONFLICT

Conflict is at the heart of modern fiction. People who tell you that one region of the world or another doesn't tell stories with conflict is full of it - conflict doesn't have to be overt, physical, or based around sex, guns and explosions, but it's always there in some form, in every story. *The Epic of Gilgamesh*? Conflict. *Dream of the Red Chamber?* Conflict. Fables? Conflict is how the storyteller conveys the moral.

Conflict in stories is any kind of constructive tension or friction or yearning, a state of restlessness that indicates that growth is occurring in the narrative. It is not synonymous with arguing or fighting, and some of the best conflict actually occurs when characters are in agreeance and STILL in conflict over the course of the story.

How do you have conflict without arguing or fighting, you may ask? A good example is the relationship between a new couple. Have you ever heard that term, 'New Couple Energy'? It's the stage where two people have realized their attraction to each other and may be glued at the mouth, but there is still a 'feeling out' process going on under the surface. Partner A is career-driven, Partner B hates working. Partner A likes peas, Partner B hates them. Partner A loves cats, Partner B was bitten by a cat as a toddler and still has reservations. Despite this, they are 'madly in love'. In the early phases of a relationship, we tend to overlook these differences, and partners often think these kinds of things are 'cute'... but they can cause problems down the road. There's no arguing or fighting in the first bloom of love, but there is tension under the surface, and tension is conflict. You know that one day, when Partner A wants a cat and Partner B doesn't, and Partner A leverages the fact that they're the breadwinner because Partner B doesn't work and she can get a cat if she wants to, that there's going to be blood. That's conflict, too – just more overt.

Conflict is also not 'bad', and doesn't always involve 'bad' things happening to your characters, especially on the micro level. Conflict in a story is like a personal trainer, inciting your protagonists to grow, grow, grow. If they can lie around on the couch and surf Netflix with nothing stirring them on, they're not protagging very hard, are they? Conflict is an itch that creates change.

Simple conflicts tend to involve opposing forces, while more complex and subtler conflicts can be between forces that are mostly in alignment but that operate at cross-purposes. Here's some ways that you can add conflict into slow plotlines or scenes:

- Make your character's flaws a barrier to them achieving their goals. Conversely, make them have to overcome their flaws to achieve certain things.
- Everything your protagonist does can have consequences. Their actions, decisions, causes and mistakes can be leveraged for tension.
- Let your characters make mistakes: protagonists, antagonists, and secondary characters.
- Give your protagonist two motives or goals. Make them both emotionally compelling. The protagonist must sacrifice one to achieve the other.

- When faced with multiple choices, give each choice a positive and negative outcome. No choice is easy to make, and there is always a price to pay.
- What is your protagonist good at doing? Throw them the opposite of what they're best at and make them deal with it.
- Give your characters strong opinions. It doesn't matter if you like their opinions or not.
- Try not to leave your character alone too much. Give them someone or something to play off, be annoyed by, or long for. If they're alone, make sure they have something to do.
- Have things go wrong, even in improbable ways. The cheesier it is, the more comedic it will be, and this can be used to your advantage in certain kinds of stories. Remember, though, that coincidence is a one-way street. You can use it to get your protagonists into trouble, but not out of trouble. Conversely, few things are more frustrating/exciting than a stroke of luck that favors the antagonists.
- Highlight the hairline cracks in otherwise-perfect situations, such as a new romance or a victory that leaves someone out in the cold.

THE POWER OF CADENCE

"This sentence has five words. Here are five more words. Five-word sentences are fine. But several together become monotonous. Listen to what is happening. The writing is getting boring. The sound of it drones. It's like a stuck record. The ear demands some variety. Now listen. I vary the sentence length, I create music. Music. The writing

sings. It has a pleasant rhythm, a lilt, a harmony. I use short sentences. And I use sentences of medium length. And sometimes, when I am certain the reader is rested, I will engage them with a sentence of considerable length, a sentence that burns with energy and builds with all the impetus of a crescendo, the roll of the drums. The crash of the cymbals – sounds that say listen to this, it is important." - Gary Provost

One of the most important qualities of good writing – and good editing – is cadence. Cadence is vastly overlooked in craft-of-writing books because it is not a technical quality which is often recognized by readers, though it is appreciated by them. Have you ever wondered why some writing almost seems to compel you to read on, while other lines fall completely and entirely flat?

This is why: the writing lacks cadence.

Cadence literally means 'falling', as in the falling inflection of the voice at the end of a sentence. In music, cadence is: "A progression of chords moving to a harmonic close, point of rest, or sense of resolution." (Free Online Dictionary). It is the balance and rhythm found in the best poetry and music. It is literally the way in which a combination of words sound when they're spoken aloud... or read in your mind by your internal narrator.

I cannot emphasize how significant this simple musical concept is to the craft of writing and, by extension, editing. Cadence is how you create, sustain and emphasize emotions and actions. You can use it to balance dialogue so that it becomes irresistible to read.

The quote from Gary Provost is a beautiful

example of cadence in action, but here is another demonstration: the following lines are extracts from *The Hollow Men*, a poem by T.S Eliot. Spellings are in the original British English:

We are the hollow men
We are the stuffed men
***
Shape without form, shade without colour,
Paralysed force, gesture without motion.
***

Between the desire

And the spasm

Between the potency

And the existence

Between the essence

And the descent

Falls the Shadow.

Focus on the first two lines in particular. Read them aloud and listen to your own voice. *"We are the hollow men. We are the stuffed men."*

You can almost hear the boots marching, can't you? The sharp rhythm of those sentences is brutal to the ear, the words falling like hammer blows – exactly what the poet intended. Combined with the imagery, you have a beautifully evocative image.

In my opinion, cadence is more important than perfect grammar, and your own peculiar use of cadence will define your voice, style and story like nothing else. Grammar means nothing if the work is not compelling. You know how I mentioned that some authors can get away with huge tracts of exposition for world-building purposes? They do it by turning their work into a rhythmic form that is enjoyable to the ear and mind:

"Its substance was known to me. The crawling infinity of colours, the chaos of textures that went into each strand of that eternally complex tapestry... each one resonated under the step of the dancing mad god, vibrating and sending little echoes of bravery, or hunger, or architecture, or argument, or cabbage or murder or concrete across the aether. The weft of starlings' motivations connected to the thick, sticky strand of a young thief's laugh. The fibres stretched taut and glued themselves solidly to a third line, its silk made from the angles of seven flying buttresses to a cathedral roof. The plait disappeared into the enormity of possible spaces." - China Mieville, *Perdido Street Station.*

China Mieville has confessed in interviews that he enjoys writing classic purple prose (the kind that was used in Romantic period literature, not so much the kind that is used in modern Harry Potter fanfiction), and his love affair with English is obvious in most of his work. It's not everyone's style. Neil Gaiman's subtle lyrical style, Dan Brown's direct simplicity, and William S. Burroughs' aggressive, abstract writing have all found their audiences as well.

If you're somewhat unsure as to what kinds of rhythms do what, you can figure it out by counting syllables as 'beats' when you read aloud. People think very easily in tempos comprising 4, 6 and 8 beats, and any sentence with that cadence will be read quickly. Conversely, one with an uneven number of beats will seem sharp or slow, depending on tone, length and word choice. Let's try it with an amusingly rude command to sit down:

"Sit!" = 1 beat, imperative.

"Sit down now!" = 3 beats, exaggerated imperative.

"Sit your ass down now!" = 5 beats, jagged tempo.

"Sit yourself down there." = 5 beats, slowed. Word choice and tempo soften the order.

"Sit your ass down in that chair." = 7 beats, jagged but slow. A threat.

"Sit down!" = 2 beats, imperative.

"Please, take a seat." = 4 beats. The addition of 'please' makes it easy on the ear. Contrast to the terser 3-beat 'Please sit down' or 'take a seat'.

"Sit your ass in that chair." = 6 beats. Word choice is harsh, but not as harsh as the 5.

"You sit your ass down in that chair." = 8 beats. A milder threat.

You've quite possibly heard these variations used through your lifetime, or phrases like it, with each kind used for its own special effect on the ear. We instinctively use cadence in speech to indicate our intent. "I'll pick you up at six," and "I'm coming for you. Six pm." both have very different meanings. Effective speakers, orators and speechwriters use cadence to plan their speeches for maximum impact. If you were ever called into the principal's office, you probably knew the difference between what 'Please, have a seat' and 'sit down' and what the principal's choice of words meant for you, in regards to reward or punishment. You probably didn't even think about it! You read the cadence and tone of voice in light of the context of the situation, and the combination of the two imparted understanding.

It's time to try this with your own book. Take a scene from your work – any scene which you particularly like. Now, read it aloud.

- Anywhere where your tongue trips up is a sentence that lacks cadence.
- Anywhere where an allegory or illustration seems to lack power, lacks cadence.
- Any sentence that sounds 'off' or clumsy lacks cadence.
- Any *key emotional sentence* which doesn't sufficiently evoke emotion lacks cadence. Not all sentences have to do this, but many do – and if they don't, rework the cadence.

If you're a new writer, discovering your voice via cadence can be quite a painful exercise. But note where you really do feel your voice flow, and where you do succeed in allegory, rhythm and emotion. Write more sentences like that one.

To illustrate, here's a single sentence from my own work, *Blood Hound*:

"The waiting room of Markovic, Volotsya, and Goldstein enfolded my senses with cool, perfumed solace."

This sentence could have been written any way I chose, but read it aloud and you might notice something. It's a very rhythmic cadence, broken up by a small 3-note. I wanted to convey that beautiful hush we all feel when we step out of the sun on a hot, tiresome day into a cool environment. It's that moment when the door slides closed behind you, and your sweat chills and you go: "Ahhh." It's a sense of order descending after the noisy, hot chaos of the city during Summer.

What if I had written it: "Volotsya, Goldstein and

Markovic had a cool perfumed waiting room which enfolded Alexi's senses and gave him solace?" They're nearly the same words, but in a different order they're a completely different sequence of beats. It loses the rhythm and becomes run-on.

How much of this should you check? I don't recommend getting too hung up on 'beat-counting' – your instinctive sense of how something flows when you speak it aloud is usually enough to judge whether something is worth keeping or changing. The beat-counting technique is useful for the times when common sense fails. You can use it for opening lines, ending lines, emotional, impactful moments, important dialogue, or other such hot spots. If your work reads slowly or your eyes skip a line, go back and check it for cadence. You might find that that particular paragraph is out of tune.

Cadence is also indicated by word choice and the structure of sentences. There are a bunch of different techniques which are used by masterful writers which you can apply to your own work like embellishments.

SONIC RHETORICAL DEVICES

Rhetorical devices are useful definitions for literary (or oratory) techniques which can be used by writers to create certain kinds of emphasis. They can also be used to assist in creating cadence in your work. A Google search for '30 rhetorical devices' will bring up more information, but here's a few of the most useful ones:

Polysyndeton (Po-lee-SYN-de-tun)

Polysyndeton refers to the process of using conjunctions or connecting words frequently in a sentence, placed very close to one another. A common technique is the use of and... and... and, instead of listing off items with commas. *"She was graceful and effortless and confident, poised, and when she turned to face me..."*

This technique mimics the gushing thought process which often accompanies fear, awe, or other strong, arresting emotions. It's a good way to induce catharsis.

Alliteration

Multiple words beginning with the same first letter – used sparingly, also creates a certain kind of cadence. One line of dialogue from the marvelous game *Undertale* has this technique used in it: "Prestigious! Powerful! Popular!" The context makes this dialogue really funny to read.

Amplification

A literary practice wherein the writer embellishes the sentence by adding more information to it in order to increase its worth and understandability. Gary Provost's quote illustrates amplification quite well, and Neil Gaiman is fond of this technique as well.

Anaphora (Ana-FORa)

Repetition of word or words beginning a series of parallel syntactical units ("This sceptered isle, ... this

blessed plot, this earth, this realm, this England!").
Anaphora is very good for loud and angry arguments:
"You did this! You killed him, you... you MONSTER!"

Assonance

Recurrent vowel sounds ("sweet, sleeps, creature" all
have an 'ee' sound) which can convey tone to dialogue.
Remember how I said that the adjective 'whining' is
often used by writers to convey someone is cowardly
or annoying? Rather than describe them, try
assonance to make their sentences sound whiny. "I
just need the keys, pleeeeeease! I need to get going!"

Cacophony (Ka-kof-an-ee)

The use of words with harsh consonants, usually at
the beginning of a word, e.g. KitKat, cacophony, Tic-
tac, slap, fracas. This is very useful for setting a hard-
boiled or edgy tone. Clive Barker is a master of
cacophony.

Epistrophe (Ee-pis-tro-fee)

A figure of repetition that occurs when the last word
or set of words in one sentence, clause, or phrase is
repeated one or more times at the end of successive
sentences, clauses, or phrases. "I will take this ship, I
will fly this ship, and if you don't like it, you can go
down on deck in handcuffs because it's my goddamn
ship!" The opposite of anaphora.

Simile (Si-mee-lee)

A figure of speech that expresses a resemblance

between things of different kinds (usually formed with 'like' or 'as'). Many similes are cliché nowadays ("her skin was as pale as the moon") but the basic technique is an effective and efficient way to get a key description in.

There are an awful lot of rhetorical devices out there, so pick and choose wisely. Like a thesaurus, they are best used sparingly.

You can find a list of examples here:

http://americanrhetoric.com/rhetoricaldevicesinsound.htm

LINE EDITING: THE NITTY-GRITTY

N ow that we've covered some of the big issues of line editing, let's get stuck into the finer details of good writing.

THE THREE TENSION KILLERS

We read genre fiction because we enjoy watching and experiencing characters doing exciting things, and the key word there is 'do'. We don't want exciting things to be done upon our passive and uninterested characters. We don't want our characters observing exciting things and not being involved. We certainly don't want our author telling us that their characters are doing an exciting thing over there, and because they say so it has to be true. These three things – (unintentional) passive voice, tentative phrasing, and narrative distance – are some of the biggest tension killers in writing.

Unintended passive voice, tentative phrasing, and narrative distance. These three issues can be found in every piece of writing by authors of every level of ability, self included. To understand and spot these errors, it is important to understand why these things occur in our drafts. All three relate to the process of 'feeling out'. Even the most well-planned novel requires the author to feel out blindly through each scene, chapter and section, spinning dialogue and often being surprised by the twists and turns in their own narrative. As you stretch your hands out into the dark, feeling for signposts and points of orientation, you shuffle forwards into the story. It is a rare person who can charge into a dark, unfamiliar room with full confidence. These tension killers mark the places where you were mapping out this dark space in your novel. They're normal, natural products of drafting, and they're nothing to be upset or defensive about.

Of the three, Passive Voice is probably the most familiar, most misunderstood, and least tension-killery, so we will look at that first.

THE VOICE THAT IS PASSIVE

Out of all of the arguments I've had on the Internet, I'd say about seventy percent of them were about what defines the passive voice. It's one of the things that is so frequently mistaught (and therefore, penalized or incorrectly flagged) at school that it has become a topic of deep confusion and frustration for many people.

Let's start with refresher on the two elements

you'll use to identify, fix or add in passive voice. These elements are the **subject** and the **object** of a sentence. The quick definition of these two things are that the Subject does things to the Object. Subjects act; Objects receive actions. Objects can be passive (like a ball) or active (like a puppy, or another person) or something in between.

This gives self-editors a key clue to identifying what is or isn't passive voice. The subject and object are always nouns or implied nouns. *Verbs cannot be the subject, because verbs cannot act on things by themselves.* The subject *has* to be something that has the ability to perform actions. 'Running' doesn't run down the road by itself, but Mark the Jogger can run down the road. Mark is a Subject; the road is the Object on which he performs the verb action of running.

The formal definition of what constitutes 'passive voice' effectively refers to any sentence which puts the emphasis on the object instead of the subject. In other words, the person or thing who is performing the action doesn't have an active role in the sentence. The action in a sentence is performed upon the subject:

Simple active voice: *Mark runs down the road.*

Simple passive voice: *The road was run upon by Mark.*

Another example: "The ball was played with by Jane." The ball is the object; Jane is the subject. We know this is passive because the emphasis is on the object, not the subject. This is a crudely obvious form of the passive voice, and easily corrected to an 'active' voice by switching the subject and object around so that the subject is acting on the object. "Jane played with the ball."

English is (mostly) what linguists call an SVO language: Subject, Verb, and Object in order of position. 'Mary (Subject) danced (verb) the tango (Object)'. In other words, we have a noun-verb-noun structure underpinning English sentence formation. Not all languages work this way, but English certainly does. You cannot, for example, write: "Danced the tango Mary does" outside of Star Wars fanfiction. Unless you're very clever, your readers will probably miss what you were trying to say... so unless you're intending to screw with them, you likely already avoid doing things like this. Not all languages use this structure. Navajo (along with 45 percent of the world's languages) uses a SOV pattern of Subject-Object-Verb: "Mary (the) tango danced." Irish uses a VSO form: "Danced Mary the tango."

Using the SVO structure in English provides a 'clean', logical, quick reading experience. Active sentences seem dynamic because an action is being performed, and an English-speaking reader's eye will follow these sentences at maximum speed. This can be quite lyrical and/or creepy: "It puts the lotion on its skin, or it gets the hose again." Strong SVO/active sentences are not created at the expense of cadence.

Does this mean you should scrub the passive voice from every part of your novel? Absolutely not. There are times when the passive voice is ideal, but they are the times where you *intentionally* want or need to slow down a sentence. This is why, at this beginning of this chapter, I note that *unintentional passive voice* is the tension killer. Effective use of the passive voice can heighten suspense. Remember that suspense is related to uncertainty, and uncertainty can be created by drawing out time. Passive voice can lend uncertainty to an action.

Passive voice can appear in any sentence with a subject or object performing an action, internal or external:

"The thought occurred to him." 'He' is the logical subject of the sentence. Emphasis is on the object, the thought that belongs to the man. We want to emphasize the gravity of his thinking.

"This castle was built by the witch in a day and a night!" cackled the old hag. (There's two-for-one.)

"The sword (o) swung down in Sir Pantsalot's hands (s), cleaving the ogre's skull." How do we know the sword is the object? It has no impetus on its own. It relies on its wielder, the subject, to do something. Emphasis is on the object, because we want to flash the lurid image of the blade slicing the orc's head.

"Perhaps a questioning might be in order?" The acolyte leaned forward. His voice was level, even pleasant, but his eyes gleamed black in the rippling light of the fire. Passive dialogue, active action.

All of those examples contain the passive voice. Note how in all cases, the subject of the sentence is dominated by the object? These sentences could be edited into the following active forms:

"He thought."

"The witch built that castle in a day and a night!" The old hag cackled.

"Sir Pantsalot's sword cleaved the ogre's skull."

"Perhaps we should question him?" The acolyte leaned forward.

You get the gist. As you may note, none of those active

examples are necessarily 'better' than their passive counterparts.

Passive voice lends itself very well to slow, poetic, intentional cadence, and also to speech or thought that has to do with slyness and general skullduggery. Because it slows down the reader's eye, passive structuring can be used to spool tension out into a paragraph. That last good passive example with the acolyte shows a time when the passive voice adds to tension. *"We should question him."*, would be a grammatically active form of *"Perhaps a questioning might be in order?"*, but it would also destroy the acolyte's subtle aura of sadistic menace.

Usually, however, you don't *want* to slow down. Hence the tension-killing part. If someone has to read back and forth to make sense of who is kicking whose ass and in what order, you turn a potentially exciting scene into a ho-hum event. "The gun was pulled by Alexi just in time to aim it at the head of the mobster," is a shitty passive sentence.

Another use for the passive voice is if you're writing non-fiction, or styling bits of fiction to read like non-fiction. You don't always want to emphasize the subject in non-fiction. This can be the case if the subject of the sentence is an unknown actor/personage. "John F. Kennedy was assassinated in 1963 by an unknown gunman." That is passive voice – yes, really. JFK is the object – the one who is being shot – by the subject, the gunman.

In contrast, "An unknown gunman shot John F. Kennedy in 1963," sounds a bit... throwaway. Even though the shooter is the subject and the President the object of the action, why would we emphasize this unknown 'somebody' over the important figure of John

F. Kennedy in this sentence? The target of the assassination is the natural focus of the sentence, and the passive voice gives gravity to the action that was performed.

Problems with passive voice occur when you need an active sentence to convey quick, dynamic action. Any fight, any conflict (and there's a lot of that in fiction), sex, motion or other activity usually does better when it's in active voice. In most writing situations, you will lean on the active rather than the passive voice because the active voice is more forceful and precise. In genre fiction, you want to be forceful and precise as much as possible – hence the often-heard throwaway advice to cut passivity out of your novels without exception.

Here's an exercise. Let's edit a paragraph to remove passive voice, so you can get a bit of practice in spotting where it is best to remove and replace, and where it might be appropriate to leave passive voice intact:

Last year, my village was pulled into the war by the new King. It was the Imperial Army vanguard, and much damage was caused by their outriders, mounted on huge beasts with mouths full of razor teeth. The wheat in the fields was burned and eaten. Fires raged across the roof of our neighbor's house, the thatch set alight by flaming arrows. The market was flooded with soldiers and sacked. My mother and the children hid in the cellar while we guarded the windows. When we began to think that the worst was over, we heard a loud scream and looked out the window to see that they were dragging people behind their chariots towards the village square. It was the mayor and her husband! Gods, if only we had listened to the refugees. If I'd known this is what would have happened, I'd have made sure our family would have been the first to leave.

Rewrite this paragraph in active voice, and see what difference it makes. Then, change some sentences back. Do any of them look better when they're passive? Why, or why not?

The kinds of passive sentences you'll probably need to replace in your manuscript sound clumsy and slow when you read them out aloud. You have to contort the language around the meaning of the sentence, rather than use it to embody the action you're trying to perform. "The axe whirled in the hands of Sir Pantsalot's foe, who was grunting as he levelled his blade at the knight's face," is a lot harder to write (and read) than: "As the knight stumbled back to his feet, the orc swung the axe down at Sir Pantsalot's face."

Like every rule of English, passive voice can be used for effect. When it comes to the SVO order, treat it as a law for the most part. You can and should screw with it if appropriate, especially with dialogue. Yoda's unique pattern of speech and his enduring appeal are fine examples of how flexible the rules of English really are. The key is always *deliberate action.*

'Was'

Let's get something straight. One thing that is NOT passive voice is the use of 'was' in a sentence. 'Was' does not indicate passive voice, okay? It doesn't. 'Was' refers to past tense. It *can* be found in passive sentence structures, but by itself, it is not indicative of passive voice. I have seen this particular argument many times over many years while participating on groups and forums online, but it is an irrefutable and concrete law of the language that *was* (or any form of the verb 'to be') does not, by itself, create a passive sentence.

The 'was doing' (or was... -ing) construct is NOT passive voice. It is progressive past tense, which shows an action continuing at a point in the past:

"Bob rested." = Past tense (simple)

"Bob was resting." = Past tense (progressive)

Neither of those are passive. How do we know? In both instances, Bob is the subject, and he is doing the resting.

The following sentences *are* passive:

"The resting was done by Bob." = Past tense, passive voice.

"The resting had been done by Bob." = Passive voice, past perfect tense.

How do we know? Because Bob is being referred to as the object of the sentence. Easy.

Progressive past appears in more complex sentences, as well:

"Bourke hit the ground rolling, and snatched the gun from the floor." – Active; uses both progressive and final past tense.

"The gun was snatched by Burke from the floor as he hit the ground rolling." – Passive.

"Burke had hit the ground rolling, and had snatched the gun from the floor." – Perfect past tense (technically not passive, but still kind of meh. Often mistaken for passive voice).

The reason that 'was' is equated with passive voice is demonstrated in the second-last example. There has to be a 'to be' verb linking the object, action and subject, because they are out of their natural order. More often than not, that linking word is 'was'. But 'was' does not make the sentence passive.

Make sense? If you're writing a story in past tense, you're going to find yourself using both the simple and progressive (and occasionally, the perfect) forms, especially if you are including more than one action in any given sentence. If people try to tell you that your progressive actions in the past tense are some form of passive voice, you now have the ammunition to fire back.

TENTATIVE CLAUSES

Unlike passive voice, there's no good reason for authors to make use of tentative clauses outside of dialogue. They're bad and you should feel bad for using them.

Tentative clauses are one of the simplest and most overlooked problems in writing. They usually occur in descriptions, but also pop up during observations and other kinds of action. Finding and eradicating them is incredibly satisfying. Like pimples, they are small and unattractive markers just begging to be squeezed and eradicated. Unlike pimples, clearing them from your manuscript will not create a new cluster of them, and will greatly improve your flow, pace and cadence.

A tentative clause is part of a sentence which suggests something instead of stating it. It is an *incredibly* common mistake. If you are a writer who began writing through online role playing, your writing is nearly guaranteed to be full of tentative clauses, because they are frequently used in RP to avoid god-moding or directing other character's actions. They are also major tension killers.

For example, here's one I ripped from an online channel where I role-play: *"The Ranger stepped inside the bar, venturing to look around the room. It was dark, smoky, and the bar seemed to be made of black wood."*

You see that 'seemed' there? This is where you put on your Samuel L Jackson voice, point your gun at it and yell: "IS THE BAR MADE OF BLACK WOOD OR NOT, M*****F****R?"

"The orcs seemed to be getting closer." Are they getting closer, or aren't they?

"She would offer a soft smile, hoping that he would understand." ARRGH.

"I wondered if she-" NO. NO WONDERING FOR YOU. BAD WRITER. NO BISCUIT.

Any word which allows room for uncertainty – *seem, could, should, maybe, might, wondered, pondered, considered, probably* – should be mercilessly pruned from your work whenever possible.

Please note that tentative clauses are not the same as actions which just happen to be tentative in nature. "She crept to the doorway and peered around the edge," is fine; "She used her stealth to creep to the door, hoping that the occupants within could not hear her," is tentative.

If your sentence indicates that something may or may not happen, change it so that either the thing happens or doesn't happen, is or isn't real. Eradicate uncertainty. If the suggestion is fuzzy, the reader will not have a clear picture and the power of that sentence is decreased. The only place to ask questions or express uncertainty is dialogue, and even there... if it doesn't add to the scene, don't use it. It's better to lie about the result of an action (as in, the POV characters thinks something happened when it didn't) than to tentatively suggest that something might happen.

'Better' and 'best' are also often tentative, and so are words like them. For example: "My Dark Arts teacher gave us some examples so that the class could better understand the dangers of necromancy."

It's kind of posh sounding, but also stealthily tentative. Do they understand, or don't they?

Another kind of tentative clause are sentence that begin with 'had'. "Had he gone into the library, he would have seen the butler with his tray." Did he go in the library or not? Why are we being shown something that someone didn't actually do? These are common in oldy-worldy narratives, but aren't very good unless you're writing Victorian-style fiction or you're really committed to omniscient third-person.

Now, for the grammar enthusiasts out there: If you want to get technical, there is no such thing as a single 'tentative clause' in English grammar. It's a term I made up to describe the use of several different kinds of clause, which includes verb-first, SV and some kinds of declarative clauses. I group them together because the details are beyond the scope of this book and will distract you from self-editing. The important part of editing them is get rid of the uncertainty and the air of 'suggestion' which these constructs create. Once you spot a few, you'll start to see them everywhere. As you get rid of them, your writing will sharpen into focus.

NARRATIVE DISTANCE

Also called 'narrative imposition', narrative distance is a particular problem for third-person perspectives. First-person authors struggle with it as well, but it is more pernicious and harder to spot in first-person. It's related to narrative imposition, and in some circumstances, they are one and the same thing.

When we write in the third-person, we generally imagine our scenes to be something like a movie: a sequence of images, actions and interactions spiked with emotion and color. Because most people tend to 'see' their book as they write it, they also tend to interject their God-like viewpoint into the narrative. Sometimes, you cannot help but do this. If you're writing third-person past tense, you do have to say things like: "Jason turned and glared at the Paladin." The author is literally describing this from their third-person perspective, but they're describing something the audience can see.

The problem is when this sentence continues: "Jason turned and glared at the Paladin. *Look at him standing there, shining in his armor*, he thought. <u>He wondered if the paladin was judging him.</u>"

That underlined last sentence there evokes narrative distance. In the first part of the example above, we see Jason turn. He thinks; we hear his voice, as if he was speaking. But then, we leave Jason's voice, and we hear the voice of the author saying: "He wondered if the paladin was judging him." Is that something you do in your daily interactions? Do you think something, then step back and self-narrate: "And having made my order at the counter, James Osiris Baldwin thought: is my barista experienced enough to prepare my fat free pumpkin-soy-whatacino with creamy whip?"

The key to sorting out narrative distance is this: If the action is internal to the character or subject (the do'er) of the action, don't describe them performing the action. Just make them do the thing without telling us that they're doing it. *Look at him standing there, shining in his armor*, he thought. *Bastard's probably judging me over all sorts of shit."*

Here's another example: "Karel didn't notice the pain in his legs, the trembling ache that spoke of knotted muscles. All that he cared about was Lydia."

Sounds nice at first read-through, but if Karel didn't notice the pain in his legs, who is telling us about the pain in his legs? And what is that 'spoke' doing there? What is speaking? 'All he cared about was Lydia'. But where is the actual evidence of caring? And who is telling us he cares? It's shallow, lazy prose.

Also, do you see the 'that' in that sentence? 'That' often lives within meta-narratives and slow sentences. One useful little trick: run a search for 'that' and read what turns up. You'll probably have to do quite a lot of reading – I've seen manuscripts with thousands of instances of 'that'. It's worth the slog: 'That' is often one of the key tells for narrative distance and other narrative imposition issues, especially when combined with a physical or emotional action verb. "That he cared", "that she wrote," "that spoke of". 'That' is one of those danger words you should always pay attention to while editing. It generally doesn't need to be there.

If you're watching a movie where the action was interrupted by an unseen narrator telling the audience that Nicolas Cage was thinking, would you really believe them? The best third-person narrative is the narrative which fools the reader into thinking that the author is not there. The author creates the illusion that the readers themselves are generating the images, voices and emotions in the story. Some people use narrative distance in an attempt to be clever, but it really just comes off as smarmy. It ruins suspense. "Blissfully unaware that my partner had just resigned, I followed my morning routine." Why tell us that when you could launch us into the character discovering that his partner has gone? It's like spoiling the end of a book.

If you're writing in first-person, the impact of narrative distance is even greater. A third-person author can get away with it sometimes (George R. R Martin gets away with it a lot), but a first-person narrative has to maintain closeness. 'I thought', 'I saw', 'I ate': these are all impositions of an artificial presence. Try interacting with things the way your character does, and see how many times you really use 'I' outside of conversations and internal dialogue. You might tell someone else "I'm going to the kitchen to fix some coffee," but rarely will you ponder: "My head hurts and I need coffee, so I'm going to the kitchen now." You'll just note the aching head, think 'ugh' and go to the kitchen, no narration needed. How to write that kind of natural process into fiction?

Significant imposition: *"**I noticed** my head was hurting: **that** meant it was time for caffeine. "Hey babe, hang on for a couple of minutes," **I said**. "I'll go fix some coffee."*

*I **searched for the door and** made my way upstairs to the kitchen to **look for the coffee pot**. It was on the counter **as always**.*

Minimal imposition: "My head was pounding: it

was definitely time for caffeine. "Hey babe, hang on a couple minutes. I'll go fix some coffee."

I made my way upstairs to the kitchen and set the pot on."

'I made my way upstairs' isn't really an imposition in first-person, because it is an action – you could find another way to word if you wanted, but it remains invisible enough to pass. We still have to orientate the reader somehow, but it's far less intrusive than an artificial 'I looked for/I did x' narrative. The 'that' is highlighted for reasons explained earlier in this chapter.

So that's it – your three tension killers. Cull your soggy tentative clauses, remove excess passive voice, and remove narrative distance. Read back through, and bask in the sudden increase in the power and emotional impact of your writing... because in fiction, emotions are king.

WEAK WORDS

"Instead of characters knowing anything, you must now present the details that allow the reader to know them. Instead of a character wanting something, you must now describe the thing so that the reader wants it."
– Chuck Palahniuk

Thought verbs – wondering, pondering, dreaming, thinking – are weak words. When someone wonders, knows, thinks or remembers, you're automatically putting distance in between the character and the reader. You don't sit there thinking to yourself about how you're thinking to yourself. This is called 'metanarrative', and is avoided in strong writing.

Meta-narrative is a short-cut, which is why we tend to write it in while drafting – we don't know the story ourselves until we've written it. Line editing is where you have to find these truncated meta-narrative parts, and unspool them into descriptive prose.

Chuck Palahniuk wrote an amazing essay on this subject, and to be honest, anything I could write in this book was already written by him. You can read it here: https://litreactor.com/essays/chuck-palahniuk/nuts-and-bolts-%E2%80%9Cthought%E2%80%9D-verbs.

CHECKING FOR AND STRENGTHENING EMOTIONAL POWER IN SCENES

Entertainment is popular because of how it makes us feel. Intellectually, we may be fascinated by good worldbuilding or the complex characters and conflicting moral systems in our favorite novels but, at our core, we are all hormone-fueled, emotion-driven meatbags looking for a thrill. Intellectual interest is motivated by emotional payoff, and so in practice, your book can flaunt every rule of English grammar (with the possible exception of evil perfect tense) and still be a best-seller. If the writing is emotionally arousing and compelling, no one will particularly care about your grammar until after they've finished reading. Your work doesn't need to be perfect or clever or new – it needs to be emotionally captivating, for yourself and for other people.

Emotion is why technically mediocre writers (or even really bad writers) can sell very well, while brilliant but stylistic writers can languish in the slush pile. Like it or not, humans respond to emotional triggers. We are very easily manipulated by feelings. There's a reason all genre fiction basically boils down a cocktail of sex, excitement, fear, pain, death and desire. This is one of the major reasons I encourage writers – and editors – to not beat themselves up over failing to attain an ideal of perfection. The more you think dry, technical thoughts about a work of art, the greater the risk of stripping the emotion from it.

Editing for emotion is tricky. Over-editing your manuscript puts you at serious risk of scrubbing the feels out of your writing. Emotion is dirty. It is messy and many-hued. If you try to wash out the color to 'make it better' or less challenging, or less confrontational, you will feel something slip away from your work. Strong emotion helps to carry a scene, and you omit it at your peril. If you kickstart your book on a flagrant emotional high (or low), you have a much better chance of hooking your reader. But how?

Here are my Editing for Emotional Impact rules-of-thumb.

Edit for scene appropriateness

If your character is giggling flirtatiously during what is supposed to be a traumatic combat scene, chances are you haven't nailed the right emotional cues in your work. Is the emotion expressed in a given scene the emotion you want to evoke in the reader? Does the emotion suit the scene, setting, and character?

You want to make sure the emotions you depict

are immediately relevant to what's happening. That can be anything from simple expressions, such as a young character crying at a difficult moment, to complex, subtle reactions, such as the dazed, vacant smile of a soldier who's just seen his buddy get his head chopped off by a helicopter rotor blade.

This is more an art than a science. If you aren't certain your scene is hitting the mark, wait until give it to your First Reader and ask them how it makes them feel. What do they think is happening here? Be careful not to load your questions, because if you ask someone something like: "Does this make you feel happy" or "Is this an intense scene?" they are likely to give you a biased answer to try and please (or displease) you.

Trust your instincts, not your inner professor

Emotion is instinctual – we rarely think about what we're feeling while we're feeling it. If you read a sad section of your book and feel sorrowful, chances are your reader will, too. If you read a sad section of your book and think: "Hmm, this is the sad scene, I better make good on that hair-tearing," it's likely that your scene has missed hitting the emotional trigger. A simple scene which makes your readers grieve for the characters will win out over a clever little commentary on the transient quality of human nature every single time. Intellectualizing emotional moments in stories tends to come off as snide or dull.

If you're an intellectual person by nature or have issues with expressing emotional affect (as many autistic people do), I would suggest that you work on identifying any scenes which seem to trivialize something that you know should be emotional. Print them out, set them beside you, and listen to some music that evokes a particular emotion for you. While listening (or just after), write NEW scenes *longhand* in a notebook, focusing on turning them into emotionally compelling micro-scenes. How you go about this depends on your writer's voice, but try to stick to the visceral more than the mental. You should be able to work through the block.

If your eyes skim past it, it's not emotionally compelling

One trick to detect the drying up of emotion is mark where your eyes skim over while reading. This is also a great way of picking up drops in tension of any sort, but it's particularly important while gauging emotion. If you find yourself skipping over something, there's a good chance it's not hitting the emotional reward switch.

If the paragraph/scene is *meant* to be emotionally engaging, it needs to be revised. If it's not an emotional moment – a paragraph of exposition, say – check it for flow and speed, focusing on cadence, passive voice, and perfect tense.

Edit for power and flow

Emotional scenes are most captivating when they work like a rip-tide, overwhelming the reader and submersing them in feeling. Take, for example, the opening of Vladimir Nabokov's Lolita:

"Lolita, light of my life, fire of my loins. My sin, my

soul. *Lo-lee-ta: the tip of the tongue taking a trip of three steps down the palate to tap, at three, on the teeth. Lo. Lee. Ta.*

She was Lo, plain Lo, in the morning, standing four feet ten in one sock. She was Lola in slacks. She was Dolly at school. She was Dolores on the dotted line. But in my arms she was always Lolita."

Nabokov perfectly evoked the child-like, frantic appeal of Humbert Humbert. For those who haven't read it, *Lolita* is the POV character's prison confession, and Humbert is an unreliable narrator. He's a pedophile, and his immature infatuation with Lolita is raw to the point of being saccharine. In an effort to gain our sympathy, the character ripped out his beating heart and holds it up to the reader in offering. The many responses to this plea over the years have seen Lolita lauded, banned, burned and beloved in turn. Love it or hate it, Nabokov definitely knew how to push buttons.

Beware of purple prose

Cadence may be an important part of writing, but like any writer's tool, too much of it is never a good thing. The modern definition of purple prose is writing that is so ornate, flowery and drama-tastic that it draws excessive attention to itself, rather than keeping the reader in the story. *The Elements of Style* says that purple prose is: "hard to digest, generally unwholesome, and sometimes nauseating."

Purple prose is basically description on methamphetamines. It's characterized by overuse of the things that make writing beautiful under other circumstances, including adjectives, meaningless (or 'zombie') nouns, and superfluous metaphors with only a tenuous relationship to what is being described. Fantasy and romance are especially prone to it, but I recently read (or tried to read) an urban fantasy that had an unfortunate amount of purple prose.

Ideally, you want to strike a balance between completely dull and utilitarian (brown?) prose and fancier prose that shows off your voice. Consider the following:

Plain: *"Sir Pantsalot cut off the orc's head."*

Blah, who cares? This sentence sounds like he's going to the bathroom, or getting a sandwich.

Fancy: *"Sir Pantsalot dodged the axe blow, rolling underneath the orc's outstretched arms, and came up with a slashing blow of his sword. It took the monster's head off, and he threw himself to the side as the corpse toppled forward towards him."*

This one hits the spot for me – a Goldilocks Zone with enough description to be dynamic, but not so much as to get wrapped up in itself. Your taste may vary.

Too fancy: *"With his hair flaming like the sunset over a dying planet, Sir Pantsalot danced forward with his silver rune-etched blade which glowed with a virile white light, his golden blazing orbs full of fire and as he opened the orc's neck like a treasure chest, spilling forth a foul shower of life fluids like rubies covered in slime."*

Literary meth – not even once.

You can avoid purple prose by using the words you need to use, not the words that sound pretty but have no intrinsic relationship to what you're trying to describe. At best, you make a laughingstock out of your scene; at worst, you come across as being pretentious and masturbatory. The exception is if you're going for a certain kind of humor that uses purple prose to build up hilarity.

Unfortunately, many purple prose authors think they're the bee's knees, that their writing is perfect, and never actually seek to change or learn anything. I sincerely hope you are not one of those people.

Emotion vs drama

If we shift from purple prose to what generally inspires people to purple-up in the first place, we come to the relationship between emotion, drama, and melodrama. Emotion and drama are often bedfellows, but they're not the same.

Drama is action intended to cause an emotional response; the emotional state is what affects the reader. One of the most infamous examples of drama without emotion is surely *The Room*, a film directed by the infamous Tommy Wiseau which is widely believed to be the best-worst film ever made. *You're tearing me apart, Lisa!*

Conversely, you can have profound emotional impact without drama. *The Handmaid's Tale* by Margaret Atwood is a story which relies heavily on the inner emotional world of the protagonist. There are relatively few moments of drama in that book, and the Handmaid's environment often makes external drama impossible. Some of the most intense scenes of the novel occur with the protagonist alone in her bare bedroom.

Just as drama without emotion is passionless and trite, too much pure emotion without any action is dreary and can make people squirm with discomfort.

This is where we get melodrama, which is where the experience of emotion is turned into a dramatic action. Melodrama is where the sobbing widow slides down the banister, smearing it with tears and saliva, then falls down the stairs and rolls around at the bottom crying her little heart out... for three pages. With very few exceptions, it fits into the 'too fancy' category.

Remember how I warned you to critically examine any 'sitting and thinking' scenes in your novel? Much in-character thinking is intended to elicit emotion, but even the most beautiful prose can become dull if a character languishes in a black hole of rumination, self-pity and inactivity. Inner monologues are a prime culprit for emotional false-starts, especially for those of you writing in first-person. This is in part because inner monologues often come across as being self-absorbed and pointless. The story is often better served by having the character doing something or interacting with another character or the environment. Even the Handmaid wanders around her room, discovering the secrets of the house while she languishes in the boredom inherent in domestic slavery.

Cadence is an important tool for creating emotional impact. Here are some fast tips on how to use rhythm to effect emotions:

- To create a sense of speed in your writing, remove or replace words that slow it down. Use hard consonants and short words, and make use of cacophony or other rhetorical devices that 'chop up' your sentence.
- To slow down a sentence and build tension, add words. Experiment with passive voice, anaphora, etc.

- To increase intensity, use 'power' words that evoke a strong response in the reader ('lust', 'kill', 'blood', etc.) and make sentences shorter, with staccato cadence.
- To decrease intensity, use 'stringing' words that are vowel heavy, make sentences longer and the cadence more 'looping'. Use longer sentences.

The following lines (third-person omniscient) make use of all of these techniques. See if you can identify them:

"Salvo was almost under the fence when the soldier turned. Their eyes met. As they stared hopelessly at one another, the Red Army's machine guns rattled in the distance; the muddy ground steamed around them in the weird, pregnant silence.

Then the enemy bought his rifle around and the bubble of space shattered. Neither man could say who fired first."

THE USE OF 'SAID' AND OTHER (AD)VERBS

Many experienced readers – agents, editors, reviewers, educated members of your audience – will criticize the use of adverbs other than 'said' (and a handful of others) to sign dialogue and action. There's a good reason for this: adverbs are lazy. Like all the 'rules', it can and probably should be broken at times, but not everyone is going to have the same success as adverb-happy authors like Patrick Rothfuss.

Because they are 'telling-words', adverbs are best

used sparingly. When it comes to dialogue, 'said' and 'asked' are your workhorses, with occasional ventures into words like 'whispered', 'replied', 'grunted' and other quick descriptive terms. However, even 'said' can be intrusive or monotone, especially when used without any other dialogue signposts. Dialogue is best when it is contextualized by action, and the rhythm you create between action, speech, adverbs of speech and scene breaks is a very important part of developing your voice.

There are two basic core guidelines for using 'said', or any other adverbial signifier of speech.

#1 – Place 'said' and adverbs in a logical order.

Just to reiterate, English is an SVO language. To minimize the presence of telling-words, put the subject first. Some authors use 'said <Character>' instead of '<Character said>', but this is an old convention and is rapidly aging. 'Said X' was used in the Victorian Era and is weightier than 'X said', which is why some people like it. *"I am here!" said the Prince.*

I admit that this happens to be a pet peeve of mine, but think about it. 'X' is the noun and 'Said' is the verb ('to say'). In modern English, 'said' should typically come after the Subject. In other circumstances, you wouldn't write something like: "Danced X the Tango."

As much as I hate to admit it, this isn't a hard rule. The 'X said' structure is common in some types of stories, and it can give a 'fairytale' or Period vibe to a piece of work. This is fine if you're writing epic fantasy: not so much if you're writing science-fiction, military fiction, or a postmodern thriller. *"You get your filthy maggot ass to the parade ground right now!" said the drill sergeant.* Eh. It doesn't really work.

Combining illogical verbs and adverbs is another common issue in draft manuscripts. 'Smiled softly', for example. A smile is a visual thing; softness is predominantly tactile. Choose something else visual or an abstract emotional state which is able to be read from the face. Speaking softly? You 'feel' that quality of softness in your ears, so it's logical.

'Growled angrily' is an example of illogical adverbial usage. What is a growl if not an angry or aggressive sound? Can you 'growl cheerfully'? Why does the author clarify?

Here's one I saw in a manuscript in 2014: 'Snarled jokingly'. This doesn't make much sense at all, and it sounds clumsy when you read it aloud.

Be smart with adverbs and descriptions. A smile that reaches the eyes, growling (with no modifier), and a short portrait of a character's sardonic snarky tone of voice would be better substitutes for those three examples.

#2 – Balance narrator indications of speech with character actions

It's not a good idea to have characters performing an action after every piece of dialogue. There's only so many times someone can pace, light a cigarette, wave their hands, or cross their arms in a conversation. The goal is to make it clear who is speaking, and to characterize the person speaking to the best of your ability within the limits of the scene. Have actions when appropriate and rely on the context of the dialogue. A good guide for pacing action and use of 'said' in an exchange is to look for the natural pauses in the conversation, and then tag the next person to speak.

Anna crossed her arms, and a thick silence descended over the table. Paul sighed.

"Seriously," **he said**, *"I just want to talk. So please, talk to me."*

One problem with dialogue occurs when the author tries to reinforce something someone is saying by specifically pointing out the obvious:

"I'm sorry," he apologized.

"Absolutely not!" he argued disagreeably.

When someone says 'I'm sorry', we already know they're apologizing. Fix those up with accompanying actions instead of tells.

It is my personal opinion is that the only adverbs to use for speech are those which actually *involve the delivery of speech*. These are words like said, whispered, muttered, murmured, shouted, asked, etc. Anything else, and you begin to impose on the physics of the human body. 'Laughing' is not a way of delivering speech. Neither is smiling, grunting, coughing or leering. 'Barking' and 'snarling' are (borderline) possible, but best used judiciously. Try to 'smile' your next piece of dialogue out loud. You can smile until your cheeks burn, but you won't be able to express words that way without looking really weird.

A very Australian demonstration of why adverbs suck

To further elaborate on the way in which adverbs cheapen your work, let's look at the following examples where adverbs destroy nuance.

One of the most commonly used terms of address in Australia is the word 'mate'. This one word is like a mini-language unto itself. We use it kind of like the word 'buddy' in American English, but we use it everywhere and for everyone. 'Mate' can be (and is) used for friends, enemies, police officers, strangers, your boss, your subordinate, the guy on the phone... each address with different tones of voice and in different contexts. The way you use the word with a friendly workmate is totally different to the way you use it on some drunk mongrel who's hitting on your girlfriend at a bar.

Were you to try and write these nuances that accompany 'mate' with adverbs, it would look like this:

"Hey, how's it going, mate?" Blue said cheerfully.

"Hey! Mate! Watch where you're going!" Shazza exclaimed angrily.

"Hey! Mate! Watch where you're going!" Matty cried fearfully.

Notice a pattern? All tell, all the time. They're really flat.

Compare the above with the same lines, but delivered with activity instead of adverbs:

Grinning like a shark, Blue slapped Pete on the back as he settled on his seat at the bar. "Hey, how's it going, mate?"

"Hey! Mate! Watch where you're going!" Shazza flung

his middle finger up through the open window, leaning the heel of his hand onto the horn.

Oh shit. The guy was going to go right off the side of the building if he didn't stop. Matty ran for him, waving his arm. "Hey! Mate! Watch where you're going!"

The expressions are now vivid and contextual. This phenomenon is very relevant for when you're trying to deliver a cultural, social or emotional context with your writing.

As you line edit, I recommend you examine your dialogue cues, tags and general adverb (and verb) usage to determine if your choice is creating the writing that you want, or if it is filling in for something that should be more complex and exciting.

VAGUE SENTENCES AND THAT OTHER THING

There is a huge difference between creatively suggesting ambiguity or complexity, and writing a vague sentence that means nothing. A writer will sometimes try and write someone experiencing a cluster of subtle feelings, which instead comes out as being a mess which typically ends in 'that'.

This is a real life example I saw in a manuscript once upon a time: *"He wanted to laugh, but it was as though he'd be stuck without that."*

What does that even mean? He wanted to do something? Why doesn't he do it? Why 'as though'? Be stuck without what? Laughter? The only thing he is 'stuck without' is meaning.

Run a search for 'as though' and other similarly ambiguous terms. Weed them out. Judge if you were trying to capture a cluster of subtle emotions or actions, and strive to describe the outcomes rather than tell us the source. Communicating complex emotion is possible, but it requires some very specific description:

"His face rippled with a smile that quickly faded, followed by the light in his eyes. He shuffled for a moment, then jammed his hands in his pockets before turning away to mask the tension of his face."

If a sentence has appropriate cadence and perfectly suits that scene, leave in something short. Not every action has to be expounded on, but if you find 'that's and 'as thoughs' and 'as if's masquerading as nuance, you are going to have to weed out the lazy writing and give your readers something to chew on.

YOUR COMPUTER'S MAGICAL READ-ALOUD FEATURE

Modern technology is a glorious thing. Even more glorious is the ability of computers to help you read your work. Reading aloud does so many awesome things for your work that I probably could have dedicated an entire section to it, but here are a few of the reasons why you need to do it:

- Reading aloud quickly reveals what sentences or scenes don't grip you, the writer, and which are almost certain not to grip any of your readers.

- You turn up repeated words, run on sentences, and other easily corrected mistakes.
- If you tune out to something while reading aloud, you know you've hit a dead zone in your work.
- It helps you refine your style and voice.
- It helps dialogue sound natural and authentic.

To help you spot all of these things we've talked about, you'll have to read your work aloud or have someone – or something – read it out for you.

There are main three ways to do a read-aloud and use it for editing. The first option is, naturally, to read it out loud yourself. The second option is to have someone else (or a recording) read it to you. The third is to have the computer read it aloud, and for this stage of editing, it is the last that we will be looking at. Most of you will be able to do this with one of two programs already on your computer: Adobe Reader and Microsoft Word.

Adobe Reader text-to-speech

Adobe Reader comes with a really neat text-to-speech feature which allows you to import a file as a PDF and then have a somewhat flat but efficient voice read the text aloud to you. The voice factors in punctuation and is generally very thorough. You can convert your text document to PDF by saving it as a PDF file in OpenOffice or LibreOffice (or Word or Scrivener). Here, you will learn how to do it step by step. I highly recommend you work with your read-alouds one chunk at a time at this stage of editing and don't try to do the whole thing at once.

First, separate the chapters you want to edit in a new file. In Microsoft Office, you go to File > Export > Create a PDF/XPS document. In LibreOffice, you click the 'Convert to PDF button', or go to File > Export as PDF:

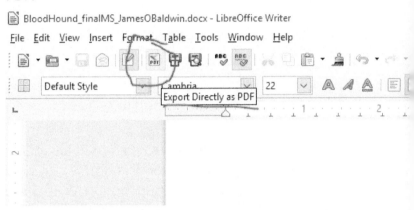

Once you're in Adobe Reader, you don't need to change any of the default options to access the text-to-speech function.

Navigate to the top level menu and select View. At the bottom of the View menu, you will see 'Read Out Loud'. Click that, and click 'Activate Read Out Loud'. You can also just press Shift+Ctrl+Y to do the same thing:

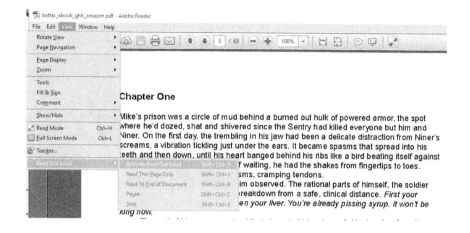

Once you've selected Activate Read Out Loud, navigate to the Read Out Loud menu a second time, and you will see you have several options:

You can deactivate the read out loud mode, read to the end of a single page, or read the entire document. You can also use the select tool in Adobe Reader to highlight a paragraph or sentence, and the program will read the highlighted text and stop. The single page and highlight features are very useful for line editing and copy editing, while the whole document read is better suited to proofreading and substantive editing.

Microsoft Word text-to-speech

If you haven't done it before, enabling text to speech in Word is a bit more complicated than using Adobe Reader, but it is advantageous because you can directly edit your document while you listen. Word uses the same flat voice as Adobe Reader.

If you've never used the Text-to-Speech function in Word before, the first thing you have to do is enable the shortcut in the quick menu. Open up the menu (which looks like a line with a little arrow pointing down) and select 'More Commands'.

On the menu, select 'All Commands' from the dropdown. Scroll down until you find 'Speak':

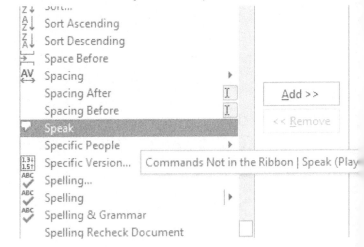

Click 'Add' to add the speak function to your quick menu and hit 'Okay'.

Now, the speak icon (a speech bubble with a right-pointing arrow) will be available in Word. It will normally appear shaded and be unselectable. To use it, highlight the text you want it to read. The menu item will light up, and when you click it, the program will begin to read aloud.

Once you've enabled text-to-speech in Word, it will always be available. All you have to do is highlight what you want it to read, and then click the quick menu icon.

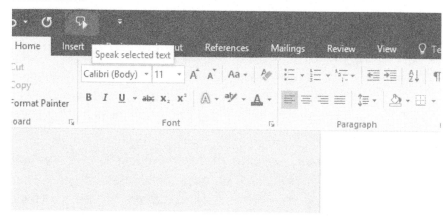

Some people may find that the read-aloud features don't work on their computer. You can probably download a text-to-speech install or update from the Microsoft or Adobe websites, or find some other way of getting it on Linux or Mac. You have other options, though, the foremost of which is to record yourself reading your book aloud and then listen to the playback. This isn't a bad idea anyway, especially if you're specifically editing for cadence. It can be harder to hear cadence in your computer's robo-voice.

DIALOGUE

I don't actually have a whole lot to say about dialogue, because what constitutes 'good' dialogue is intensely subjective. Dialogue is the most flexible part of writing, and it is, perhaps, the most flexible and characteristic element of a good novel. Just as we like some people and hate others, what one reader finds charming and funny annoys the piss out of someone else.

What you can do during this phase is edit your dialogue with the rest of this chapter (and the last) in mind. Give your characters a distinctive voice. Cut out adverbs and substitute them with actions or supporting illustration. Make use of cadence. Make use of strategic passive voice, or remove passive voice and tighten it up. Play with accents, word choice, and wit. Dialogue generally benefits from fluff-cutting even more than prose.

There's a couple of basic guidelines with writing dialogue. The first is that the rules of grammar absolutely do not apply to dialogue, ever. Basic sentence structure does, sure, but everything else is fair game. Written or spoken, it doesn't matter. You want your character to speak entirely in clichés for a line? Do it. Perfect tense? If they really want to. Blathering word salad? Why not?

The second guideline is that, no matter how unintelligible or wacky your dialogue becomes, assign each speaker a new paragraph. But we already covered that.

One common problem with dialogue in draft manuscripts is that all the characters can come off sounding the same. Everyone has a unique way of speaking. One of the most basic differences is vocabulary size. Personally, I've read a lot of books where some thuggish guy is noted by the POV character/protagonist as 'having the vocabulary of a brick/barn/truck/tank/other manly dumb thing.' Rather than tell us this, show us your character struggling for words in the course of their dialogue, or have them misunderstand or fail to understand something said by a wordier character. The reverse also applies.

One issue that isn't so substantive is the way that foreign words are used in dialogue. You have to make sure that the meaning of those words is clear to a reader who doesn't understand that language. You can do this through brief (very brief) exposition by dialogue, or through context.

The formatting used for different kinds of dialogue – spoken, written, foreign and internal – is covered in the copy editing chapter.

Dialogue is one of the places in your book that the text-to-speech function will let you down. There is no robot reader in existence which can properly capture the inflection of dialogue. As you review and revise, read every single piece of dialogue aloud word for word. Be careful of skipping or hyphenating words aloud when you have spelled them out in the text. Ideally, your dialogue will sound like slightly truncated, but real conversation. If it's stilted, slow, or clumsy, reword it.

MISCELLANEOUS LINE EDITING ISSUES

As you do your read-alouds and plug through your manuscript, here's a few other things to keep an eye out for as you continue to line edit:

- **Time:** Does time in your book make sense? If your hero wakes up on a Monday and fights the big boss on Wednesday, did everything really happen in two days? Make sure that dates and times are correct, fictional or otherwise. I recommend the Time and Date Calendar for managing this: http://www.timeanddate.com/calendar/

- **Place:** Are places named consistently? Nations? Hotels? Bars?
- **Names:** Are character names consistent? If a character has nicknames, are these nicknames used in such a way that we know which character they refer to?
- **Voice:** Do your characters speak in ways that make their voices recognizable?
- **Style:** Are you happy with your own voice/narrative style, and is it reasonably consistent throughout the book?
- **Motive:** Do the actors in your story have sufficient motives for what they do?
- **Details of clothing, setting and scene:** are these congruent throughout your story? Does the heroine have black hair in the beginning of the story and blond at the end?
- **Technical details:** The make and model of weapons, guns, procedures, quoted facts... double check every detail you've had to research for your novel and decide on your level of realism. We know, for example, that silencers don't actually completely suppress the sound of a pistol. If your book is more theatric, creative license can and should apply; if it's more realistic, make sure your depictions are factual.
- **Plotlines:** Are your plotlines congruent and resolved? If a plot is intended to span over

more than one book, do you somehow sign that this is a continuing mystery or event?

- **Dialogue:** Is your dialogue snappy and fluent when read aloud? Have you omitted superfluous dialogue? Have you replaced lazy adverbs with action whenever possible?

COPY EDITING: A QUICK AND DIRTY GUIDE

Congratulations! If you made it this far, it means you're well on the way to finishing your damn book. The developmental and line editing processes are much, much harder and more time consuming than copy editing will ever be. However, be warned: copy editing is, in a word, dull. Perhaps because it is so dull, some people get really anal over it. There is an entire book written by a guy named David Crystal on the use of exclamation marks, I shit you not.

Perhaps because of the conflict that copy editing seems to bring on, many writers fear this stage the most. There's some validity to this – copy editing is the most technical phase of editing and is the stage where you can make definite errors. However, copy editing is pretty easy when you have a reference and pursue editing with congruency (not perfection) in mind.

Strong copy editing has recently become a vital skill for self-published authors. Amazon recently implemented a new system where readers can report errors in the books they read. The error count in a book is publically displayed on the book's page, meaning that significant copy editing errors can hurt your sales. If you're submitting your work, literary agents and readers will turn their noses up at manuscripts with spelling mistakes or simple grammatical errors, often dismissing otherwise good stories due to shoddy copy editing. Sad but true.

Copy editing is the stage where you need to decide on a style (as in, editorial style) and stick to it. If you're submitting your work to an agent or publisher and they have a particular style guide preference, you're best off adhering to their style.

No matter what style you use, you can and will have to stand your ground against the hordes of internet trolls who eagerly tell you that your use of 'was' indicates passive voice (it doesn't), or that periods should always be set outside of quotation marks (they don't) and that you are a lesser being if you didn't catch every smartquote in your book. Get used to it – everyone's a critic in the literary world.

WHAT IS COPY EDITING?

'Copy', in this instance, doesn't mean 'to imitate'. 'Copy' is the industry term for text scheduled for publication. A blog post is copy. A magazine or newspaper article is copy. Your manuscript is copy.

A piece of copy is, specifically, a *finished* article, blog post or manuscript. The process of writing copy is called copywriting or drafting, and the process of finalizing copy is called copy editing. So what you're really doing at this stage of editing is finalizing your manuscript, getting it ready for submission to agents or for publication. For copy editing to be most effective, you must do it after everything else is finished!

The first thing to do, then, is to go back and make sure you are happy with your manuscript after the developmental and line editing phases. If not, rest your book for a couple of days, and go over it again quickly with your planners until you're satisfied that it is ready for the window dressing.

Here are some of my top tips for effective copy editing:

- Keep a dictionary (online or hardcopy) on hand at all times while copy editing. If you're using a defined style guide, have it on hand.
- Read this section in its entirety before you touch your manuscript. You're going to have to look for lots of different things at the same time, on every page. It will help if you know what you're looking for before you start.
- If your eyes start swimming or you feel fatigued, take a break. Trying to copy edit when you're tired is really hard.
- Get some chewing gum, candy, or some kind of lozenge. It's much easier to edit with something to keep your mouth busy, hence the stereotype of the chain-smoking newspaper editor. I chew my way through at least a dozen pen caps a year.
- Avoid alcohol or anything that reduces your executive function, including lots of sugar.

'Write drunk, edit sober' has some validity, particularly at this stage, for the same reasons that driving drunk is inadvisable. You lose your ability to notice details.

- A bit of caffeine can help you feel sharper. Too much will make it impossible to concentrate. If you don't do caffeine, B vitamins and L-Carnitine (a common supplement used by body builders to increase metabolism) both work very well alone or in combination. I personally use all three.

- Increase your font size. Most writing programs allow you to scale your page, artificially increasing the font size without actually changing it. Even if you have good vision, copy editing at 120-140% zoom will help you focus on each sentence as you read it.

- Change the font of your manuscript. If you were using a sans-serif font like Arial, consider changing to something with serifs for copy editing. If you drafted in a serif font, choose another serif font for the copy editing phase. Make sure your font clearly distinguishes between letters, punctuation marks (including hyphens and longer dashes), and quotation marks of various kinds. My favorite font for copy editing is Georgia.

- If you don't have a comfortable workstation, I recommend working on hard copy first. It's easy to miss things when your back or wrists are hurting.

FORMATTING YOUR MANUSCRIPT FOR COPY EDITING

The goal of copy editing is two-fold: to proofread all of your line editing changes and make sure they're properly meshed into the bulk of the text, and to catch mistakes at the word and sentence level. These include but are not limited to: spelling mistakes, grammatical errors, punctuation, incorrect word usage, tentative clauses (again), word order, double negatives, and page formatting errors. The copy editing stage is concerned with fine details. Once you've finished copy editing, your manuscript will have reached the 'what you see is what you get' stage... at least until your beta readers and book-buddies tear it apart.

There are as many ways to optimize the copy editing process as there are editors. Nearly every editor has their own personal methods for managing the challenges of this stage of editing: eye strain, mental fatigue and typo-blindness. This book uses my preferred system for copy editing, but you should tinker with it until you find the way that works best for you. This is measurable, of course: if doing things one way leaves you with more mistakes than doing it another way, you know what works and what doesn't.

The first stage is formatting. This is the point where we doll up your manuscript for submission (to agents, or an editor), or publication. Up until this stage, we have been working with a manuscript in draft form. We now have to get it ready for other people.

Standard manuscript format

If you are submitting to a specific person, place or publication, they will have a preferred manuscript format. They will typically publish guidelines on their website, if you adhere to the submission guidelines of the people you are contacting, you can count yourself in the top 5% of their slush pile. As a former slush-pile reader, I can assure you that very few people actually pay attention to agency/publication formatting guidelines, and any editor or literary agency reader will be grateful that you put in the effort.

If you don't have a specific place to send your work, then the best practice is to format your manuscript in a generally accepted style. Often referred to as the Shunn Format, the details are as follows:

- 12pt font.
- Double spacing between lines.
- One space after a full-stop.
- Courier font (though you can usually use Times New Roman or Georgia, too).
- 1 inch margins all around.
- Page numbers, Author Surname, and book title in top right header, each divided by a straight line (the |) or right-forward slash.
- Chapters begin in the middle of a new page (use page breaks to separate chapters!)
- Minimal caps.
- No spaces between paragraphs.
- 0.5 or 0.3-inch indent at beginning of each new paragraph.
- Titles are 24pt, subtitles are 18pt, chapter headings are 14pt.

You can see an example of a correctly formatted manuscript here: http://www.shunn.net/format/novel.html

Preparing a manuscript for self-publishing is far more complex. If you're self-publishing, I suggest that you copyedit in a format that approximates the standard manuscript format in the word-editor of your choice. There are programs you can use to format ebooks in XML, but they often have very rudimentary spelling and grammar software, if any. I do not recommend trying to copy edit in those programs.

Once you've formatted your manuscript in this manner, we can move on to the next step: macro-editing. If you prefer to work on a printed manuscript, I recommend you hold off on printing until after this step. The kinds of errors you will be looking for can be easily fixed by the Find and Replace function in Word and OpenOffice/LibreOffice, so you might as well nab them before you commit the manuscript to ink and paper.

MACRO-EDITING: BULK CORRECTIONS FOR SMALL MISTAKES

There are certain kinds of small mistakes which are commonly found throughout a manuscript. In this section, you'll learn how to find and fix them.

First, select your entire document (Ctrl + A) and change the language to your preferred region. Yes, even if you're pretty sure you've written in one variant of English this entire time. If you've copied and pasted anything into your manuscript at any point, you might have stray paragraphs or sentences that contain a different English variant. Your spellings should be consistent with either your country of origin, or the country of the publishers/agents you are submitting to.

Once you've done that, here is the checklist for the second phase of copy editing: correcting bulk mistakes.

- Run a spell check[2]. Make sure you program your new words and names into your dictionary during this first big check. It's fairly common for character names to be spelled inconsistently throughout the course of a draft manuscript. This step helps you find where you might have done this.

- Check all character names. Are they spelled exactly the same way? Check all place names, countries, item names, etc.

- Check all suspect words against a dictionary, even if spellcheck says they're correct.

- Run a second spell check. Make sure nothing comes up.

- Make sure all proper nouns are capitalized.

- Search for the weapons your character uses. Is

---

[2] *Note: When you run a spell check and add in your new terms, make sure that you keep a consistent style with hyphens. Automatic spell-checkers love hyphens for some reason, and will want to add them into all your contractions (like 'copywriting'. It will want to turn it into 'copy-writing'). These hyphens are not always correct.*

their pistol the same caliber as last time?

- Actually, search for any unique item, spell, power or talent your character uses. Are they part of the same stable of abilities?

Don't worry too much about Word's grammar checker: the Microsoft grammar tool is awful and is consistently incorrect. There are no good automatic grammar checkers for fiction as of 2016, and that includes the ones you download and pay for.

Your next step is to go into the *Find and Replace Tool*. In the 'Find' field, press the spacebar twice to create a blank double space. In the Replace field, hit space once to create a single blank space. Click 'replace all'. This will catch and replace all of your accidental double spaces. If you get any hits, click 'replace all' again. You will likely have a few more that are caught. Those were your triple spaces, which are now gone!

By the way, double spaces after a period is obsolete. In the past, it was common for manuscripts to have two spaces before the capital of a sentence because of the way typewriters set font. If you're not using a typewriter, do not put two spaces at the beginning of a sentence. If you're used to double spaces and use them for your working drafts, remove them before you submit to your agent or publisher.

Also run the find and replace tool on double periods (..) and commas (,,), double conjunctions ('the the', 'and and' 'but but', etc.) and other similar small double-and-triple-up words and punctuation.

CHUNKING FOR COPY EDITING

Once you've finished abusing the Find and Replace Tool, it is time to chunk your manuscript for copy editing. This is the point where you can print your manuscript if you prefer to mark up in hard copy.

Because you're not dealing with plot and cadence at this stage, you don't need to divide your manuscript along the same lines as your plot planners. Instead, you need to divide your manuscript into a number of even pieces. How big should each piece be? That depends on how quickly you can copy edit. I personally find that 3-6 chapters (around 20 pages) is a reasonable copy editing goal per session, but you may prefer to do more or less depending on your publication schedule and personal goals. The idea is to break your book into whatever size pieces are most comfortable to work with, even if you only want to do one chapter a day. Make that your daily goal and chunk your manuscript into individual chapters, or blocks of three or five chapters... it doesn't matter.

At this stage of editing, you are quite possibly pretty tired of looking at your manuscript. I prefer to do my own copy editing in a very particular order, which might also work for you. My first chunk is ALWAYS the first two chapters. They have to be as perfect as I can get them, so I do those when I am freshest. Then, I go straight to the Beginning of the End (refer to your Plot Planner) and edit *backwards* until I reach the middle of the book. Then I do the first half of the middle, and then I do the end.

Why? If you start at the beginning and plug on through, you will find your energy beginning to wane around the Beginning of the End. Most people are most motivated to plow through the beginning and end of their book, but as we discussed earlier, the second half of the middle is ideally the most energetic part of the novel. If you're tired and can't bear to keep reading and editing because you've already waded through 200 pages looking for stray italics, it's likely that your reader's energy will begin to flag around this point. If you start from this point of your manuscript while you're fresh, you'll have more energy to put in later.

EVIL PERFECT TENSE

Do you recall my brief tirade on perfect tense in the passive voice section? Here is where we will expound on its many evils.

Perfect tense is often mistaken for the passive voice because it's slow. Slooooooow. Perfect tense is the tense that describes a 'perfected' action – something that **has happened** in the past, **will happen** in the future, or **is happening** now. Those bold/italicized terms are themselves exemplary of simple perfect tense. "I had eggs for breakfast. Now I'm having juice." That's perfect tense.

Perfect tense can also suppose that something will definitely happen in the future or that something definitely happened in the past. It takes a concept, lays it like a brick in a wall, and then mortars it down.

We need perfect tense to be able to describe definite events across the span of time. That's what tenses do – they indicate the time that something happens relative to the present moment. In dialogue, your characters are going to have refer to hypothetical past, present or future events. But when it comes to *prose,* perfect tense is a problem because it dramatically slows down the pacing of a sentence. It also relies on clumsy phrasing, such as 'had had', 'would have had', 'will have had' etc. Like tentative clauses, the use of perfect tenses tends to come about in writing when an author is feeling out the story and isn't certain what someone or something should be doing or saying. They block out each action blindly, groping for a hypothetical, and it results in perfect tense.

Go through your manuscript and remove as much past, present or future perfect tense as possible. Turn those sentences into simpler, more dynamic constructs. Instead of: "He had taken the gun from his bedside table", try "He took the gun from his bedside table."

If you search for 'had', 'have', 'would have', 'will have' and other similar strings, you will be able to find most of your perfect tense sentences without trouble. Remember that some of them are tricksy: "He should have done that before he did this" is still perfect tense!

Times when it is appropriate to use perfect tense are when someone has to interact with or refer back to a specific event in the past. For example, if you're writing a detective looking around a crime scene, some perfect tense is to be expected. *"The bloody handprints went from kitchen to ballroom. My god: **she had dragged herself all that way**?"*

Past perfect

The past perfect tense indicates that an action was completed (finished or 'perfected') at some point in the past before something else started to happen.

Past perfect tense is usually formed with the past tense form of "to have" (had) plus the past-tense form of the verb in a sentence: "I had gone for a run before I had breakfast."

To change it to active past tense, you'd write: "I went for a run before breakfast." Or "Before I ate breakfast, I went for a run."

Another problem with past perfect is its tendency to 'stack' moments in time. The alert for this occurrence is 'had had', either sequentially or consecutively (like the 'had run… had breakfast' example above). You may sometimes find yourself writing something like: "I had gone for a run before I **had had** breakfast." You are stacking two past events while enacting a present event. If you discover a sentence in your prose that needs 'had had' to function, rewrite that sentence into active past if possible.

Present Perfect and Future Perfect

Present and future perfect refer to actions that are completed in the present moment, or that will be completed in the future:

*"She **has grown** at least a foot since she turned twelve." (present perfect)*

*"I **will get** to you as soon as I'm done with this guy over here." (present perfect)*

*"Most students **will have taken** sixty credits by the time they graduate." (future perfect)*

You may note that these examples actually read pretty well. That was intentional on my part. Despite how much I hate perfect tense, like all parts of language, it's nothing more or less than a tool in the author's toolkit. Even if 99 times out of 100 it slows your narrative down and you have to change it, you'll always find exceptions. The novel format is really not very forgiving of heavy perfect tense usage, though. When you're trying to entertain, you want your actions to *happen* instead of writing about how it *did happen*, *is happening*, or *will be happening* in the future.

GENERAL TENSE ISSUES (NOT INCLUSIVE OF PERFECT TENSE)

To reiterate: tense is the temporal perspective of your writing. Past, present, future. Regardless of what point of view or tense (past, present or future) you have written your book in, you should check it for continuity of tense. Even the best writers accidentally switch tenses while drafting.

Past tense is the most common tense in fiction, followed by present tense. Future tense is hardly used at all (though it can be used with a second-person POV). Your narrative prose should be in one tense; your dialogue can range in tense depending on the requirements of the scene.

At risk of sounding really obvious, create congruent tense structure by making sure you use past-words for past tense (*was, did, stood*), present-words for present tense (*is, does, stand*) and future words for future tense (*will, do, stand*). Simple enough, if English is your first language.

It comes more complicated when you start adding

in various tense forms. "He was running" is a form of past tense (progressive past tense), as is "he ran" (simple past) and "running for the door, Dave threw himself to the ground and rolled." Past tense, all of them – even though 'running' appears to be in the present tense.

Present tense has similar challenges. "He's running", "he runs", and "running for the door, Dave throws himself to the ground and rolls." These are all happening in the present moment.

And future tense? "He will run," and "He'll be running," or "He'll run."

There's no way to write the 'Dave throws himself on the ground' sentence in future tense without resorting to future perfect tense, because we're talking about a concrete action that will be completed in the future, right? "Dave will throw himself to the ground while running and roll." You see how that has to suppose that this will take place in the future? Future tense is kind of weird, which is why we generally don't use it in fiction.

As an FYI, there are tenses which better suit certain perspectives in fiction. Third-person perspectives naturally marry best with past tense, while second and first-person do well with either past or present tense. Future tense is, in my editorial opinion, best saved for dialogue.

What does changing tense between prose and dialogue look like in practice? For example, let's say your book is third-person intimate, past tense, and a character needs to talk about something in her future. *'Siobhan stared at the map of the battlefield, then pointed at one of the enemy markers. "That can't be right. Our scouts saw them on the opposite ridge last night.*

Tomorrow, we <u>must</u> move the second legion west, or they'll catch us unawares."

Now, remember how I mentioned the perils of relying on amateur editors to read your work in the early stages of a manuscript? English tense is so complicated that amateurs always mix it up. People will often try to correct sentences like the one with Dave in it, because they see that '-ing' ending on 'running' and assume it is only able to be used in present tense. This is not true. In grammar-speak, infinitive verbs like that are called participles, and they're a totally valid part of past tense. The action expressed by 'running' happened in the past, at the same time that Dave throwing himself to the floor also happened. You can even use perfect past tense with an infinitive: "He had been running."

SOUNDS AND EFFECTS

Imitating a sound by phonetically recreating it is called *onomatopoeia* (on-no-ma-toe-pee-a). It's another potentially useful rhetorical device, but imitating sounds in writing outside of children's books and comics is tricky. More often than not, the reader will interpret the sound in a totally different way than what you experience. Some basic and widely-used onomatopoeic words are fine, but should be used sparingly:

Bad option: *BANG! KAPOW!* The door exploded out into the foyer.

Better option: *BRRROOOM!* The door exploded outwards into the foyer.

Better option: There was a moment's whining

silence before the door was sucked out into the foyer in a deafening blast of flame and smoke.

The first example not only uses onomatopoeia – it also employs clichés. If you're writing out your sound effects, they should ideally not be actual words, or the reader will say them in their head.

Either of the latter two sentences work, depending on your style and the kind of book you're writing. If your book is comic-themed or styled in some way like a graphic novel (with or without actual pictures), you can probably get away with more of these if you make it clear that it's part of the style of the book.

Speaking of clichés...

CLICHÉS

Clichés ('clee-shay', not 'clitch') are expressions that have been used so much that they've become trite, irritating, and essentially meaningless. Some clichés simply express a truism which has no reason to be expressed, like: 'the rain was wet as it fell on the ground'. 'Raining cats and dogs', 'all that jazz', and 'absolute power corrupts absolutely' are all examples of clichés.

Clichés can be used to good comedic effect when they are playfully subverted for humor or descriptions. Used unintentionally, they can make for some really cringeworthy reading. The use of clichés in writing is generally considered a mark of inexperience by the people in publishing.

If you think you might have used some clichés without meaning to, here's a reference list of common English clichés you can use to check against:

http://clichesite.com/alpha_list.asp?which=lett+1

Descriptions are a particular danger for cliché abuse. They are commonly used in purple prose (see Line Editing). 'Raven locks' and 'sapphire orbs', 'rosy cheeks', 'blond bombshell'. You get the gist.

THE BASICS

Here are a bunch of miscellaneous copy editing things to look out for, in addition to the above:

- Is each sentence clear and complete?
- Can any short, choppy sentences be improved by combining them?
- Can any long, awkward sentences be improved by breaking them down into shorter units and recombining them?
- Can any wordy sentences be made more concise?
- Can any run-on sentences be more effectively broken up?
- Does each verb agree with its subject? (See Micro-Editing)
- Are all verb forms correct and consistent?
- Do pronouns refer clearly to the appropriate nouns?
- Do all modifying words and phrases refer clearly to the words they are intended to modify?
- Is each word in the story appropriate and effective?
- Is each word spelled correctly?

- Is the punctuation correct?
- Is tense consistent?
- Is point of view consistent and well signed?

MICRO-EDITING CHECKLIST

Now that we've got all those bigger issues out of the way, we get into the tiny things. This section of the book is in alphabetical order for easy reference: a list of nitty-gritty editorial duties commonly found when editing fiction.

The sample sentences in this section aren't intended to be good – I've used the simplest and/or funniest sentence I can to illustrate the point when required.

'Affect' vs 'Effect'

'Affect' means 'to influence'. You can use it in place of 'to influence' in a sentence, or to indicate a state of

197

action without real feeling:

"I was affected by (influenced by) the President's speech."

"The princess was affecting grief, but based on our conversation last night, I knew she was happy her father was dead."

'Effect' is a bit subtler. It's used to indicate some kind of result, but can also refer to real or deeply felt emotions:

"I was effected (emotionally moved) by the President's speech."

"The effects of the King's death were felt across the land." (a result)

If you're not sure which one you need to use, try replacing the suspect word with the expression 'influenced by'. If that works as a substitute, 'affect' is probably what you're looking for. If 'a/the result' works better, try 'effect'.

Abstract vs concrete measurements

Some words refer to *concrete concepts*, which are physical or, at least, able to be measured. Other words refer to *abstract concepts*, which are not things that can be easily defined, measured, or quantified. A great many words can be both concrete or abstract depending on their usage, and you will have to measure them differently.

Love, for example, is both abstract (when used as a concept) and concrete ("My love is on a ship"). How you refer to it in writing depends on whether you're using it as an abstract verb or as a concrete noun. 'To love' is abstract; 'my love' is usually a person or thing.

Abstract verbs can be possessed (I'm hoping Kayle's love for me will be enough) but cannot be measured in discrete quantities ("I have five hopes") unless they're referring to something concrete. If an abstract noun does stand in for something concrete, use the typical unit of measurement you would use for that thing. "Five gallons of apple cider" can become "Five gallons of deliciousness" if the reader knows the context. This is a common trope in advertising copy, where marketers want to equate a positive abstract experience (freedom, pleasure, ecstasy, luxury) with a product.

If the 'hope' in question is something concrete, like a planet or a person, you could write it as: "I have one hope. That hope is the Alliance."

If an abstract concept can be measured in the moment, you can refer to plural forms. "We still have our hopes and dreams."

If using an abstract noun for its intended purpose, use the singular form: 'We can only hope' or 'I love him!'

Accents

If your written accents are too hard for an unfamiliar reader to understand, this is a problem. It's generally better to convey an accent through word selection than excessive apostrophes and broken sentences or words: too much novelty interrupts the flow of dialogue. Using *'dis'* instead of *'this'* might be more accurate for some accents, but overdoing patois (especially if you have multiple characters with different accents) impedes understanding.

Copy editing for accents, by default, will be a bit non-standard. Let's hypothesize you have a pirate character with a thick accent who is very drunk. You could render it completely phonetically and true to ear for a hundred pages, but that would make you an asshole:

"Wot I sed wuz, I mean I sez it wuz a farkin' white whale, big ol' bitch the size of me grandaddy's schooner..."

To make it to make it more suitable for other unfamiliar people to understand, clean it up a bit and add in some narrative to evoke the character's heavy slur:

"Wot I said it was, was a farkin' white while the size of me grandaddy's old ship, and a big old bitch of a ship that was." Captain Patois leaned forwards, and I leaned back. He was slurring every other word, and even at arm's length, I could smell the combination of rum and rotten teeth.

You still get a great sense of who the man is, but without the re-reading that an impenetrable accent requires.

Agreement of subject and verb

Subject-verb agreement simply means the subject of a sentence and any accompanying verbs must agree in number. This means that both either need to be singular, or both need to be plural.

Just to be annoying, words that end with 'a' often appear to be singular but are really plural, such as the word 'data' (the singular is 'datum').

This example has 'data' as the subject:

Incorrect: *The data indicate that Louise was at fault.*

Correct: *The data indicates/indicated that Louise was at fault.*

Why is Louise not the subject? Because the data is the one indicating something. Even if Louise is the protagonist of the story, she is not taking an action in this sentence.

Amused vs bemused

When you're **amused**, something is funny. When you're **bemused**, something is confusing. You are quite possibly still bemused by subject-verb agreement.

Brackets (parentheses)

Brackets/parentheses should be avoided as much as possible in fiction. You can get away with it in some kinds of novels (expository, experimental, some first-person point-of-view books), but they tend to annoy readers and editors if used too often or at all. You especially should never use them during dialogue unless you're planning to break the fourth wall. Replace them with commas or em-dashes. Brackets in non-fiction are fine (within reason).

Changing person

If there's a change in who's speaking, thinking or acting, make a new paragraph. If the same person is speaking for quite a while, take natural paragraph breaks regularly. You have to break up speeches into their natural paragraphs. This is the correct format for dialogue:

"Have you got everything, our Highness?"

"Yes, I think so; thank you," Prince Nigel looked up and over. "Except, oh… maybe not. Where's my waterskin? The one full of brandy?"

Dear God. This is going to be a long journey. Sir Martin the Long-Suffering rubbed his face. "You mean the one hanging from your pack, your Highness?"

Capitalization

Some publishers are okay with capitals for emphasis, and some are not. Every style guide has its own rules on this one, so you need to follow your heart on the matter. If you prefer caps to italics, use them consistently. Conventionally, you use italics for emphasis instead of caps, unless you are depicting something that is capitalized in the story. Signs, for example, are often capitalized. "I looked into the mine shaft and saw the warning in my headlamp. *DANGER. RADIOACTIVE.*"

Colons and Semicolons

Both colons and semicolons are much maligned in the

armchair editing world, but they have some important functions when used correctly.

Colons are used to enumerate something: you stick them at the end of a complete sentence to prove, explain, define, describe or list stuff that is related to the sentence preceding the colon.

In addition, colons are also used to demonstrate evidence or consequences of a stated fact, introduce lists of related information, or connect sub-topics with a main topic. Think of the sentence before a colon as a title, and the information after one as a sub-title. They can also be used to introduce speech, which is one of the reasons you would use it in fiction.

In American English, you capitalize the first letter after the colon. In British/Australian English, you do not. My personal preference is not to capitalize. It doesn't really matter, as long as you stick to one form.

Semicolons separate closely related items in a sentence with a slightly longer pause than a comma, allowing for a rapid change in direction in connecting interdependent statements. They are not 'colon lite': a semi-colon's strength is equal to that of a colon.

The main use for semicolons is to connect two independent statements which are related, but not enough to justify a 'run-on' effect, and which are not separated by a conjunction (such as 'and' or 'but'). For example: "My husband drinks tea; I prefer coffee."

You can also use semicolons to list lots of items when commas are not appropriate. The rule of thumb I learned was that five items or over should be listed with semi-colons instead of colons.

Commas

In theory, commas are like... English 101. In practice, the earnest self-editor will still occasionally struggle to know where to use them.

The rule of thumb with commas is this: if you need to pause momentarily while saying something, it needs a comma. More specifically, you will use a comma whenever you write an independent clause – that is, a complete unit of meaning within a sentence that features a subject and an object.

A series of independent clauses looks like this: "**I (S)** went running down **the hill (O)**, and **I (S)** caught **the tail of the dragon (O)** as it twisted around in the air."

You could feasibly make those sentences stand-alone (after getting rid of the 'and'), but you need a comma because they've been combined into the one sentence.

You also use a comma when the clauses depend on each other to form the sentence, but when each part gives some new information.

For example: "I twisted the handlebars to the front, kicked the motorcycle in gear, and rolled off the clutch." Each part of this sentence introduces something new, but action is related to the first part of the sentence.

Some of the other 'rules' of comma use you might have learned at school don't necessarily apply in fiction. It depends on the cadence and your style. For example, the standard rule is that you use commas after words like 'yes' and 'no' when they begin a sentence. However, full-stops can be very impactful when used in their place, and this is commonly used to build tension in certain styles of fiction:

She jabbed a finger at his chest. "No. You listen to me. You know we can't do this."

He looked to the side, his mouth quirked down. "Maybe. Or maybe you're full of shit."

Comma splices

Comma splices are the thorn in my side when it comes to my own work. They sound so lofty and authoritative, but they're actually a kind of style error.

Comma splices happen when you use a conjunctive adverb (*furthermore, however,* or *moreover*) to separate two independent clauses instead of using a coordinating conjunction like *'for', 'and', 'but', 'or', 'yet',* or *'so'*.

For example:

Wrong: *"There was no passage to the outside, however the adventurers were still determined to try and find a way."*

Right: *"There was no passage to the outside, but the adventurers were still determined to try and find a way."*

Or you can use a semi-colon:

Right: *"There was no passage to the outside; however, the adventurers were still determined to try and find a way."*

To find comma splices, you should look over a list of common conjunctive adverbs and identify any words you know you like lean on. Many writers love to use 'however', 'eventually', 'finally', 'next', 'therefore' and 'then'. Search these words using the Find function, but don't replace them. You just need to pay attention to the sentences they're in. If the sentences 'run on' in a stilted fashion like the first example, you need to fix it.

To fix a comma splice, you can do one of a few things:

- Change the comma to a semicolon, dash, or colon. Be careful with this one. It might fix the problem, but it is easy to overuse and can result in sentences which have exactly the same sloppy cadence.
- Turn the two parts of the sentence into separate sentences. Especially good if the original sentence is quite long.
- Replace the conjunctive adverb with a normal conjunction. 'And', 'but', etc.
- Make one clause dependent on the other. This is also tricky, because it can result in a slow sentence. In the example I gave, this would mean turning the sentence into something like: "The adventurers were still determined to find a way out, even if there was no obvious exit." Kind of clumsy, but it works for some sentences. You basically want to make it so that the second half of the sentence relies on the information you gave in the first half.

- If you want to sound very formal, you can use a semicolon and a conjunctive adverb followed by a comma. Best for official academic writing or dialogue from snotty professors.

Dashes

Ah, yes: the dreaded dash. There are three kinds of hyphens or dashes you can use in your manuscript: hyphens (-), en-dashes (–) and em-dashes (—).

Most American style guides use an unspaced em-dash for a dash between phrases. For example: "He had waited on him for hours—and that was a problem." In Australia and England, they prefer a spaced en-dash: "He had waited on him for hours – and that was a problem."

Page ranges and hyphenated words and names use small hyphens, not en-dashes (e.g. 'see pages 13-15', 'She-Ra').

In Microsoft Word, you can create an em-dash by pressing Alt+Ctrl+ the minus sign on the numberpad. You create an en-dash pressing Ctrl + the minus sign on the numberpad. The hyphen is the short dash on the main keyboard. If you struggle with this, open up the 'Insert Symbol' menu and set the dashes to the shortcut key combination of your preference.

In OpenOffice or LibreOffice, your generally create an en-dash by tapping the hyphen key twice and then space. Em-dashes take three hits to make. Your system may differ. Scrivener seems to always create em-dashes with either two or three strokes.

Double negatives

Double negatives aren't always bad, but they can be klutzy. "I'm not feeling bad," takes longer to say than: "I feel good!" They are a tool to be used for creating tension and cadence, but unwanted double negatives can clutter your story. Weed out any which aren't required.

Dreams, flashbacks and altered states of consciousness

If you absolutely must have dream sequences, use italics for the entire section, and include such sections sparingly. For an enhanced sense of tension or inevitability, consider switching to present tense. Divide them from other scenes with three centered asterisks (***):

And then, Hero McBiceps fell asleep.

***

Blah blah the Hero is dreaming. This is a dream! Insert dream sequence here.

***

Snorting, chin covered in drool, McBiceps roused from his slumber.

Having your character faint at the end of every chapter in which they are hurt is a widely abused trope (*cough*DresdenFiles*coughcough*), so be sure to vary it with conscious head trauma now and then.

Ellipses...

An ellipsis is a punctuation marker represented by three periods (...). In fiction, you're most likely to use them in the context of 'trailing off' an unfinished line of dialogue:

"I was just thinking... " Georgiana glanced at the fireplace, and then pressed her lips together. "Doesn't this all just seem a little... cold?"

Correct formatting for ellipses varies from editor to editor and style guide to style guide, so if you're wanting to conform to an established industry style (AP or MLA, for example), then I recommend you refer to that individual guide. My personal preference is to leave a space at the end of an ellipsis, as shown in the Georgiana example above.

Emphasis

Use italics for emphasis. Unless an editor asks for it, don't worry about underlining words in place of italics (including in manuscripts sent to agents: the underline thing was a typewriter convention) and pretty-much-never use bold unless you're writing non-fiction and need to highlight a word. All-caps should be used very rarely, as mentioned earlier in this chapter. If you do enjoy a good capslock rampage, use them for moments of extreme emphasis, such as screaming or shouting. They're really for your Batman-esque "MY PARENTS ARE DEAD!" moments.

Emphasis should also be supplied by a character's thoughts or emotions, implicitly or otherwise. The narrator should refrain from applying their own authorial emphasis – that's the narrative intrusion thing happening again.

For example: 'The building was *destroyed*. Where the castle once stood, there was now only jagged, gaping ruins.'

In that example, you are narrating from an expository point of view. The emphasis is yours.

The building was destroyed. Where the castle once stood, there was now only jagged, gaping ruins. Simpson stopped, staring at the ruins of his home. A jagged hole spanned almost the full width of the field. It was *enormous*.

This time, though, we have a character: the emphasis is subtly implied to come from Simpson's observation, not the author's god-like perspective.

Fractured verb phrases

Check your verb phrases (*move on, hard on, so hard, etc.*) to see if you've split them up, especially if you're using more than one verb phrase or a phrase with several words. It is very easy to write something like: "I almost let the pleasant mask I'd **worked so hard on** slip."

The phrasal verbs – 'worked on' and 'so hard' – are fractured here, split into two parts. You want to keep those words together. The correction is:

"I almost let slip the pleasant mask I'd **worked on so hard**."

This generally doesn't need to be addressed in dialogue, as we often split phrases like this in speech to emphasize something. In prose, however, it is confusing. Make sure your verb phrases are logical.

Grey vs gray

Gray and *grey* are different spellings of the same word, and both are correct. *Gray* is more common in American English, while *grey* is more common in all the other main varieties of English.

There are other words like this (*tire* and *tyre*, for example), and the 'correct' spelling depends on the variety of English you're using.

Homophones

Homophones are things like 'bear' and 'bare': words which sound the same, but which have different spellings and different meanings. They are tricky, because the eye sometimes skims over them and your spellchecker will not detect them. You have to find them manually.

If you even suspect a word is a homophone or are unsure if you're using the right word, check it against a list. You can find lists of common homophones on Google, like this one:

http://www.englishclub.com/pronunciation/homophones-list.htm

Homonyms

Homonyms are words which are spelled and pronounced the same, but which have different meanings. For example, 'row' can mean to either propel with oars, or to have an argument.

As with homophones, if you suspect that you haven't applied the right word in the right place or you aren't sure if your sentence carries an unintended meaning, check against a list.

There is a list of true homonyms you can refer to on Wikipedia:

http://www.en.wikipedia.org/wiki/List_of_true_homony ms

Indents

For most books, use 0.3 indents on the first line of a paragraph, EXCEPT the first line under a title. For example:

Chapter One

Chapter one begins.

Second line of Chapter One.

Putting an indent on the first line of a new chapter is a rookie move. Paperbacks use first line indents only. There are no spaces between paragraphs.

Italics

Use italics to emphasize key words in a bit of dialogue, for the titles of books, journals, films, plays or other created works (fictional or not!), and for foreign language excerpts.

Key dialogue: "The map. The *map*. You know, the

one we *need* to get out of this lousy hole?"

Titles: "Really. We don't have *The Tome of Becoming a Kickass Wizard in Ten Days*, okay?" The young librarian arched an eyebrow.

Foreign languages: *"Kala hab'aq! Kala!"* The woman cried out. She was already whirling the sling across her head for the throw, teeth bared.

Butch McMercenary looked aside at Token Lizardman. "Somehow, I don't think that means 'welcome to Dakhdir.'"

Some novels make use of telepathy and 'inner dialogue'. This kind of speech must be clearly delineated. Inner dialogue does not use quotation marks. Telepathic dialogue does. Both, however, use italics.

Inner Dialogue: *Dammit. I can't go on like this.* Jack sagged back on the ropes (no quotations).

Telepathy: *"Hey. I can't see you from here. Where are you?"* Jack thought, reaching his mind out to connect with Sara's (quotations).

It's and Its

Nearly everyone hates this one. Don't feel bad.

- **It's** is a contraction ("It is"). "It's a fine day for prancing, isn't it?"
- **Its** is possessive. Like 'his' or 'hers'. "Its whiskers twitched as it stared at the mouse."

Logical sentence structure

Strunk and White, in their famous editorial guide, call this particular grammatical rule: "A participle phrase at the beginning of a sentence must refer to the grammatical subject." This is fancy professor-talk for: "Your sentence must logically show how someone does something."

In other words, you want to always try and have the action being done by the right person in the right order.

Let's look at an example of an ambiguous sentence. *"Vera lunged forwards at Katya, her fist raised. A foot flashed out and she dodged, elbowing her in the ribs."*

Whose foot? Who dodged? What's happening here? One sentence might be easy enough to follow if you've got a very clear view of the characters, but a paragraph or scene of this can be impossible. You have to find a way to sign who is taking actions to avoid confusion.

"Vera lunged for Katya, her fist raised. Katya saw it coming. Her foot flashed out: Vera dodged to the side, then leaped forwards to slam her elbow into the other woman's ribs."

You have to balance speed and meaning, and make sure actions are signed to the correct actor.

Numerals/numbers

Numbers in fiction are most commonly written out

long-form: 'one' instead of '1'. Numerals are best limited, unless the numeral is significant in some way:

- "That'll be **ten** gold, miss," the shopkeep said.
- He frowned. This was the **seventh** time he'd seen the same damned puzzle.
- The sign read '**10** Arthur Street'. Yeah – this was the right address. (Note that the use of numerals refers to a literal object with certain physical features)
- "**Twenty-five** swords, and not a damn **one** is sharp enough to cut a carrot!"
- "We are the best of **Sector Eight**! We will fight!" Spacehero roared.

The Chicago Manual of Style recommends that numbers zero to one hundred be spelled out, and anything above that is written as numerals. Most other style guides recommend that zero to nine be spelled out, and 10 and above are written as numerals. This is very common in modern journalism and my personally preferred style for writing numbers.

Some people do it by spelling out one-word numbers, and numbering two-word numbers, e.g. Thirty (one word) and 89 (two words).

If you decide to use numerals, one 'hard' rule is that when a number starts a sentence, always spell it out. Consider rewording the sentence if you begin with a long number.

Round numbers above 100 can be spelled out: 'hundreds of thousands' is easier to read than 100,000s.

Quotes

All dialogue should ideally be contained within double smartquotes ("").

If you've written your manuscript in Notepad or other basic word processors, you will not have smartquotes, which can be distinguished by the curve. Regular quotation marks ("") are not curvy. If you're self-publishing, you can either have regular or smartquotes, but not both. If your manuscript has both, you want to edit out one and replace them all for consistency. Yes, this is a pain in the ass. Unfortunately, someone has to do it, and if you're self-publishing, that person is probably you.

References to things other people said generally have single quotes within dialogue, and double everywhere else. A paragraph excerpt from the book your wizard is reading will have single quotes and italics: "That's not how it says to make the punch. Look! It says: '... *mix in the lime with a liter of pineapple juice and half a bottle of rum.*' Half the bottle, man, not a quarter."

I have noticed that in American mass market paperbacks, dialogue is often set with single apostrophes instead of smartquotes. You can do this if you expect to be publishing a mass market or 'pulp' novel in the USA, but I wouldn't recommend it as a default. A publisher will set this particular feature if their house style requires it.

'S' and apostrophes: possessions and

plurals

Possessions and plurals in English are unnecessarily complicated, but fundamentally, the letter 'S' can be used to signify plurals or possession. Here's a breakdown of how to form them correctly.

Plural 'S'

- The most common way to pluralize a noun is to simply add an -s at the end. *Hamburger* (singular) becomes *hamburgers* (plural). *College* (singular) becomes *colleges* (plural).
- Nouns that end in a **vowel** followed by a -y take an -s in the plural. *Monkey* (singular) becomes *monkeys* (plural).
- Nouns that end in a **consonant** followed by a -y replace the -y with -ies. For example, *baby* (singular) becomes *babies* (plural).
- Nouns that end in a sibilant (*s, x, z, ch, sh*) pluralize by adding an -es. *Church* (singular) becomes *churches* (plural). *Punch* becomes *punches*, *hex* becomes *hexes*.
- Nouns that end in an -is are replaced by -es in the plural. *Thesis* (singular) becomes *theses* (plural). *Penis = penises*. Some people try to pluralize -is words with an '-ii' end (such as *'penii'*), but this is incorrect. Nearly all -is words are derived from Latin and have variable plural forms in Latin: the correct Latin plural would be *pēnēs*. The double -ii thing is essentially made up. If you're writing kooky dragon or shark

porn, then you're probably going to talk about a hemepenis at some point. The plural is *hemepenes.*

- 'Count nouns' that end in -f pluralize by changing to a –ves. *Calf* (singular) becomes *calves* (plural); *half* becomes *halves.*
- Nouns that end in -o preceded by a **vowel** usually pluralize by adding an –s, such as *Oreo/Oreos.* Nouns that end in -o preceded by a consonant usually pluralize with an -es. The nouns that do not follow this pattern are often words imported from other languages and take their plural form according to the rules of that language. Thus, Soprano (singular) becomes Sopranos (plural). Confusing, given that we end Latin-derived words with English-derived plural forms instead of their native plural forms... but no one ever said that English made sense.

The possessive 'S'

The possessive forms of nouns are formed by adding an apostrophe and in most cases the possessive 's'. The -'s suffix is used to show belonging: for example, Simon's coat.

Belonging can be less obvious. The expression: 'A good night's sleep' is one of those weird pluralizations. It implies that the sleeper is the possessor of the good sleep, not the night.

When in doubt about whether or not your phrase requires the possessive, turn it around and see if it breaks down into an "of the" statement. The dragon's fire (The fire of the dragon). 'A good night's sleep' (the good sleep of the [sleeper]).

You will use -'s to signify possession most of the time. You also use -'s on *names* that end with 's':

- The principal's office.
- Mrs. Jones's garden party.
- The children's bedroom.

When you have plural nouns (addicts, kids, horses) and you want to indicate possession, you use a single apostrophe:

- The horses' paddock.
- The addicts' crack den.
- The kids' playground.

If you have many people whose names end in 's', use the single apostrophe: 'A herd of the Jones' cattle galloped down the range'. You can remember it this way: "Betty **Jones's** horse is one of the **Jones'** herd."

Apostrophes should not be used with possessive pronouns (*my, yours, hers, his, its, ours*). These pronouns don't need apostrophes because they inherently show possession.

Incorrect: "That dragon is your's."

Correct: "That dragon is yours."

Signage, displays and environmental text or images

Unless there's a contextual reason otherwise, environmental text and images should be centered on the page with a blank line after. If cited in dialogue, surround with two single apostrophes OR italicize, as you would a title:

The car drew up to the old broken down gate. Rory stuck his head out the window to get a look at the sign.

WARNING. RADIOACTIVE UNICORNS AHEAD.

"Yeah, all's good, brah. This is the place," he said, and rolled the window up.

This is very much a style issue for text, but your images will look weird if they're not centered.

Sentence fragments

Sentence fragments are truncated sentences which Microsoft Word generally thinks should be replaced with a single sentence divided up by commas or conjunctions. Fragments can be used for artistic effect, as they tend to be impactful. Mix them up with longer sentences for better cadence.

Split infinitives

Separating an infinitive verb from 'to'. 'To really run' or 'to boldly go'.

They can be clumsy and awkward or impactful, depending on the word selection and placement. They're a tool to create cadence, but be wary of inadvertent usage.

Starting sentences with conjunctions

Starting sentences with *but, and, for, nor, or, etc.* This used to be a hard 'no' in Grammarland, and it's still iffy. Starting sentences with 'and' and 'but' is becoming accepted in American English. Personally, I feel they look sloppy, like an unformed thought. Unformed thoughts can be useful for certain points of view or mood requirements in fiction, however.

If you want to be strict, get rid of the conjunctions at the beginning of sentences. If you like them, leave them – just make sure they sound nice when read aloud.

The Oxford Comma

This particular comma is going out of fashion in US English, but it is still very much a consideration in UK English. These days, use of the Oxford Comma is very much a style choice. As long as you apply it consistently, you can either use it or leave it out.

If you do want to use it, here's how: In any series of three or more terms with a single conjunction like 'and' or 'but', you put a comma after each term except for the last one. For example: 'Horses, bitches, and money.'

If you write sentences where a list is so ambiguous that the meaning of the sentence is obscured, then you need an Oxford comma. If you have many items in a list, use semi-colons.

Their, They're, There

- **Their** is possessive. (Their house.)
- **They're** is a contraction ('They are')
- **There** indicates direction. (It's over there)

They/Them/Their /These

These are technically plural pronouns, but in contemporary spoken English, we generally use these as both plural and singular. Some people really hate the singular 'their', but it is now a style issue instead of being a rule.

If you're looking for some non-gender specific pronouns, they/them/their works, as does 'xie' or 'zee', but many readers still find pronouns like 'xie' too annoying or confusing to read for long. The most common title for people who go by gender-neutral pronouns is 'Mx' or 'Mixter'.

Titles (Headings)

There are two commonly accepted ways to render titles.

The standard in America is to capitalize the first letter of every word in a title or sub-title. If I had done this, then 'Signage, displays and environment' would be 'Signage, Displays and Environment'.

In Australia and Britain, it is common to capitalize the first letter of facing titles (like the titles on the cover of a book), but use normal sentence case for internal titles and sub-titles. That is the style used in *Fix Your Damn Book!*

You can use either one, depending on the sort of book you're writing and your intended audience. Web text (blogs, online stories, etc) should always capitalize the first letter in titles and subtitles.

Whose and Who's

Like it's and its, **whose** refers to the possessive, and **who's** to the contraction of 'who is'.

Possessive form: "Whose cell phone is that?"
Contraction form: "Who's that over there?"

Underlining

The style rule for underlining in novels is easy – don't do it.

The only time you *might* have to use underlining is when you want to emphasize something that is already in italics, as I have done a few times in this book. However, my recommendation for fiction is that you use caps for that word instead of underlining it.

Example: *Goddamn it. I KNEW something was going on!*

Unintended meanings

Unintended meanings occur when a phrase is misheard and rendered incorrectly. 'I could care less' doesn't make a whole lot of sense on the page. The meaning of the idiom is really 'I couldn't care less', and that's preferably how it should be written out. Other common errors are things like: "You don't misunderstand." Also see: **Double negatives**

I have occasionally seen unintentional puns in

novels. If you suspect anything of being a pun and you didn't mean to insert into your novel, change it up a little. Puns are cringeworthy at the best of times.

Wrap-up

Unless you're a magical unicorn with a photographic memory and the ability to spot a hundred details at a time, you will have to make more than one copy editing pass – and even if you can do that, you should go through a second time just in case. It may be that you focused very intently on tense and point of view on the first copyedit, and more on punctuation and capitalization on the second.

There's no set number of times you 'should' go through a manuscript in this fashion. It will vary from person to person and manuscript to manuscript. Generally, you want to remove as many errors as humanly possible, then you rest it for a while and go through one last time.

By the time you've finished all of that, you're probably heartily sick of editing, but that's okay: your work is done. For now. If you've followed all the steps in this book, you will have yourself a very nicely edited and polished little story.

Now, it's going to be up to others to help you on your way – and that is what the next chapter on beta reading and proofreading is all about.

CARE AND FEEDING OF BETAS

"Remember: when people tell you something's wrong or doesn't work for them, they are almost always right. When they tell you exactly what they think is wrong and how to fix it, they are almost always wrong." – Neil Gaiman

Betas are your friends: sometimes literally, in that they are often actual friends, but sometimes only in the sense of the service they provide. They are also volunteers, and to get the most out of your betas, I feel it is helpful to manage them as if you were the leader of a small team. But what does that entail?

Volunteers are people who are giving up their time for your cause. They aren't doing it for free, because volunteers always get something out of the work they do. Sometimes that's tangible recognition in the form of rewards; sometimes it's social capital, in the form of strengthening their relationships with you, a writer's community, their own sense of usefulness and self-worth; and sometimes it's because they are insatiable book-whores and get a kick out of reading someone's work before anyone else does. Your job, as a manager, is to determine what your particular group of betas are seeking and provide that in exchange for them giving you their hard-won free time.

Beta reading is a mutually rewarding process. Done in a spirit of friendship and community building, it is an extremely positive way to interact with people and find your first true fans.

DIFFERENT KINDS OF BETA READER

A beta is an assistant, someone who reads your work to assist you in spotting problems that you missed. Betas are your community vote. For effective editing, I recommend you try and recruit three different kinds of beta readers for different stages of your manuscript.

The first reader(s)

You probably have one of these already: a friend, a spouse, a parent, a particularly close writing buddy. They're the person you show your best dialogue to, the person (or people, sometimes) you do your whining, brainstorming, angsting and celebrating with. They're quite possibly as familiar with your story as you are, and they're the natural first audience for your manuscript. These people are probably not the most objective readers you're going to have, but they can and will provide you with an injection of confidence.

It goes without saying that if your first readers are of an abusive or crazy-making nature, you should get them out of your life.

First-step betas

The second group of betas are the people you will give your manuscript to after you have finished self-editing, but before you send it off to agents or self-publish it. Books at this stage of production are often referred to as ARCs (Advance Reading Copies).

First-step betas – ideally three or more readers – are your first real audience. You will give these readers your manuscript with the goal of finding plot holes, continuity errors, weak characters and slow scenes. If possible, you should find some betas who do not normally read your genre and who may not even 'like' your manuscript per-se. Writer's groups are made for this sort of work, and if you have one, you'll likely find them to be indispensable.

Once these guys have torn through your work, go back over it. Follow (or reject) their advice as required. If there's many problems, go over them and then have anyone willing to read over your work again do so. You will also want a few readers with fresh eyes, people you haven't tapped yet.

Second-step betas

These guys are your proofreaders. Once your manuscript is tightened up, do your final round of proofreading and hand your manuscript over to one or two second-step betas, people who can pick over the fine details of your work. This person's bias doesn't matter so much because they're looking for objective errors in the work, so a close friend or family member works fine for this step. On saying that, they should ideally be someone who has not read the manuscript before.

You need to give this person as clean a manuscript as possible. Ideally, you won't have to make any more developmental changes from here on in. Giving it to one person at a time is beneficial for the readers – if you hand it out to multiple people, they will generally come back to you with all the same typos, and collating that can be a pain in the butt. One person is able to do the job of three in this instance.

WHAT A BETA DOES AND DOESN'T DO

A lot of writers I meet online try to give betas their manuscripts before they're finished the first developmental edit. They're excited about their new work and keen to show it off and improve it. However, I'm of the firm opinion that inflicting your unedited draft manuscript on beta readers is poor form. Not only do you end up taking more of their time, you also waste your own time trying to perfect your story based on the critical opinions of other people.

Your first reader is a different story. This is usually someone close to you, like a best friend or spouse, who loves you and who is interested in sharing the writing journey with you. Some people have more than one first reader, which works out fine. These people are not going to be objective and you shouldn't expect them to be. They may be able to offer you helpful, critical advice along the way, but they lack the distance to be good critics because of their proximity to you and their emotional investment in your success. To get that critical feedback, your betas should have a bit of distance.

This means that before you email half a dozen people for beta feedback, you really need to have completed the manuscript, rested it, and self-edited. Not only does it respect the time and effort your volunteers are putting in for you, it ensures that they will be able to work on your manuscript more effectively. The mental fatigue which comes with over-familiarity is a real problem in editing. In a corporate editing team, even really good editors will tap their colleagues and swap out pieces of work with which they have become too familiar. Betas are often not professional editors and may not even realize when they're becoming overly familiar with your work. Two to three readings is about all most betas can do before they start making and skipping errors in the same places you do. It is laziness on the part of the writer to keep throwing roughly-written and half-edited work at their betas, especially if their betas are themselves writers. You should be finishing your own work: the writing AND the self-editing.

Incidentally, betas are not your editors. They are assistants helping YOU to edit your work. Unless they are themselves competent editors, readers cannot replace a third party editor. If you approach your betas as editors, they will read your manuscript with the critical mindset of an editor *whether or not they actually have the skills to edit your work*.

Because betas are your first audience, they have one of the best qualities you could hope for: they act like readers. In other words, betas pick up your work hoping for a good book, but with the willingness to point out the things that do and don't work for them. Like someone buying your work for entertainment, most people who beta read are looking for an exciting story. Their opinions in this regard are vital, and you should try to capture and distill their reader experience of your work as soon as you can.

First-step betas are indispensable for the following tasks:

- They act as your first audience and read your work in a fashion similar to a stranger picking up your book from the shelf.
- They can discuss what does and doesn't work for them.
- Their opinions will greatly assist with characterization and pacing, by highlighting

parts/personages that they skipped over or engaged with particularly strongly.

- They are great at spotting plot holes, continuity errors, logical fallacies, and inconsistent worldbuilding.
- They will occasionally pick up line editing errors and copy editing errors you may have missed. Expect some false positives, though.

Betas cannot:
- Edit your work for you (unless they're experienced editors).
- Give you a completely objective opinion.
- Copyedit (though they can and should mark up anything that is possibly a mistake).
- Work without some kind of guide to help them focus.

RECRUITING AND GUIDES

One common complaint I hear a lot online is when someone's betas "don't give good feedback." If you've sent your work to betas and not gotten useful feedback, it's usually because of one of two things:
1. You haven't finished self-editing your manuscript and have sent them what amounts to a pile of word-spaghetti heaped on a plate;
2. You haven't helped them understand what they're supposed to be looking for.

Besides that, the person you sent the work to may simply not be a good beta for various reasons. When you're scouting, you want to either recruit serious readers (people who don't write, but who enjoy reading) or writers who match or exceed your own standard of work. My experience has been that writers who do not match or exceed your standard of work are inclined to try to hands-on edit manuscripts instead of reading and flagging, and they often struggle to abide by the parameters you set for them. In their effort to be useful, they may overstep their role or give snarky/harsh critique or unhelpful praise in place of useful advice. People who are not learned enough to make informed judgements on something will make shit up in its place – this is as true of writing as it is of politics.

I personally begin recruiting my betas once my first draft is complete. I ask around, email my mailing list, and carefully screen the applicants. Some people beta multiple manuscripts because they love my work. Some people are 'once off' betas who do a fantastic job with only one manuscript (or manuscripts in one particular genre). Some people are relative strangers, but trustworthy. They are all good at the job. I will assemble preferably around five or six first-step betas and two second-step betas, though I know one person (also a professional editor) who is capable of doing both very well. I try to get a balance of readers and writers in my group.

The time I spend self-editing is also spent jotting down questions which then go on to form the basis of a *beta guide* or survey. These are queries based on the problems I noted during the developmental and line editing stages. They may relate to specific problem areas if I have places I'm concerned about. When it eventually comes time to send the manuscript off, I do a one-pass copyedit and send the text and the guide.

The guide is helpful for getting the most out of beta reading. The trick is to set the parameters you need without shaping reader bias. To that end, be sure to frame most of your questions as open questions which require the interviewee to write down something more substantial than 'yes' or 'no'. Try not frame questions with specific emotions unless absolutely necessary. "Does the character death in Chapter 8 make you feel sad?" will not be as enlightening as: "What do you feel about what happens in Chapters 7-9?"

There are two questions I ALWAYS put on the beta guide, regardless of my personal concerns. They are:

1. Did you read the story from beginning to end without pause, or did you stop at some point? If you put it down, where and why?
2. Was there anything that confused you, or that didn't make sense?

The first one in particular, despite being a closed question, is EXTREMELY important.

A really good book is hard to put down. You know the kinds of books I'm talking about – they're the ones that keep you up on a work night, joyously frustrated that you can't sleep because of its sweet siren call. If all of your betas report that they couldn't put it down, that's typically a good sign. It's harder to read any book from end to end in one sitting when you are thinking critically about it, so if your readers can't help themselves while also searching for errors, you're doing well. To check for reader bias, recruit a stranger who likes your genre (from a writer's group or crit group) and see if they say the same thing. If so, you've probably got a winner.

If your betas are enthusiastic about your book but must pause at points, you want to know where and why. Ask them to note down the EXACT place (page numbers, even paragraphs) where they stopped to do things like bathroom breaks, cooking, playing with the kids, TV, anything. If they put down your book to go and do something else, you want to mark those places and check them by reviewing your plot planner and reading aloud. Every place your betas pause to do other shit should be reviewed, no matter what they say they had to do or how inconsequential the pause may seem.

More often than not, what you will find is that your betas will pause at the same places as one another. If more than one beta sets your work down in the exact same spot, that is a huge red flag for that particular place in the book. Take the time to interview your betas about that section of the book. If all your betas put it down around the same place – say, they all stop on Chapter 20 in different places - you probably need to review that chapter. If they all stop at the end of certain chapters, rework the endings to create minicliffhangers leading into the next chapter, or make the chapter shorter and end it at a critical point.

When I was editing my novella, *God Has Heard*, four out of my six betas put the book down only once, and in every instance, it was at the end of Chapter Nine. This was a point where the two main characters finished an argument and got it on. I rewrote that section of the book based on that feedback and sent the book to three other people in my online writer's group for a simple read, no beta feedback required. None of them put it down when I changed out that 'false victory' for something more suspenseful. This is a very powerful question to ask your readers if you are trying to create a novel which commands attention.

The second question is also really important. If someone is emotionally invested in your story and you confuse them, they will get frustrated. Frustrated readers put down books to go off and feel frustrated about it. Even mild confusion means that someone has to re-read part of your book, slowing down their reading and breaking their immersion in the story. If you're writing original fiction, it is inevitable that many people won't get small instances of information and may need to go back over snippets of writing in context, but you want to minimize this behavior as much as humanly possible.

Betas are generally reading in a state of alertness, and they are very sensitive to information which they find confusing. Even if they point out something that seems obvious and easy to understand to you, take the time to pitch a rephrasing to them. This kind of thing can be hard for an author to swallow, but it's very easy to accidentally describe something in a way that makes no sense to a stranger. This is a particular risk for those abstract or immaterial innovations, like the operation of magic, technology, super-powers, or synesthesia. Fight scenes are another common offender.

Here's the guide I sent to my beta team for *God Has Heard*, the first novella I self-published.

Guide for Betas

Firstly, thanks for volunteering to beta God Has Heard for me! I really appreciate it. The editorial process is always reliant on group effort, and betas make a significant contribution to the quality of a text.

You'll get a free copy of the book for your time and trouble, and if you ever have a work you want me to look through, be sure to let me know – I'll happily reciprocate.

This doc contains some of the information I am looking for as I begin the third stage of editing. Try and hold off from skimming the questions before you read – they are more effective if you read the text first, without any critical questions in mind.

There is only one pre-reading consideration I'd ask of you: be sure to note if there is a point where you lose interest in the story and put it down to go do something else.

So... Read the Manuscript, as long as it takes, and then come back to this file and check out Page Two. Most of these questions will be best answered as soon as possible after you've finished reading the manuscript.

Love, James.

Questions!

So, now that you've read GHH all the way through, here are your questions. You can answer these here and send them back, or just number them in an email, and I'll match them up. Also, if you can't think of an answer, don't try and force one.

1) *Did you read the story from beginning to end without pause, or did you stop at some point? If so, where did you put it down, and why?*

2) *Was there anything which confused you, or which didn't make sense?*

3) *Did you notice any glaring plot holes? (If you aren't certain and think you spotted one, go back and look!)*

4) *Were there any points where your interest peaked? Which part/s?*

5) *Were there any points where your interest waned? Write 'em down.*

6) *What significant emotional responses did you have while you read? Any?*

7) *What did you think of the end of the story, specifically? Was it satisfying or frustrating? Incomplete? Rushed or not?*

8) *Were you expecting anything that didn't happen?*

9) *Conversely, did stuff happen that you didn't expect?*

10) *Any suggestions for improvement? Try and touch on anything that left you confused, frustrated, or*

wanting?

*If you notice any significant copy errors (incorrect spelling, punctuation, etc) please note them down. All spellings should be in US English."

LIMITATIONS OF BETA READERS

Without question, the most common problems I hear regarding beta reading are issues with bad feedback, lack of feedback, or non-response.

Lack of feedback is often due to the beta not knowing what they actually need to give feedback on. It can also be due to bias. In their desire to maintain a positive relationship with you, they may resort to a generic 'this is good!' response instead of giving you the feedback you need.

I personally discourage my betas from 'ripping the manuscript apart', because I consider that to be my job. If you ask someone to rip your book to pieces, many people will take that phrase on board and end up critiquing parts of the book that don't actually need to be changed, usually based on stylistic differences (especially if they themselves are writers). The human mind is negatively biased by default – people are many times more likely to report on something they don't like, compared to reporting something they do like. Your betas will do this naturally to some extent; you don't need to encourage them to start seeing problems which aren't really there.

Non-response can be due to many reasons, only

one of which is that they don't like your book. As volunteers, they have made a commitment and you are within your rights to tactfully hold them to that commitment. There's nothing wrong with checking in once a week to see how they're going: most people are even grateful for the reminder, as it helps them stay on track.

However, if there is a dull or disinterested response or the reading drags for too long past the deadline, ask that person if they really want to continue. Non-response is often due to time constraints or life circumstances, but you need a responsive team to get the best out of your work. If someone is struggling with your manuscript, try and find out the answer to the key question of 'where did you put it down?' and then relieve the pressure on that person and find someone else to take their place. It's not a bad thing or a cause for conflict, and they will likely be grateful that you had the assertiveness to relieve them of a task they couldn't complete.

A really significant reason that betas don't respond or give highly critical or negative feedback is that you haven't finished editing your manuscript before you sent it to them. If you send a finished, unedited manuscript to your readers, don't be surprised if you get dropouts. They may feel awkward about being given something that is clearly unpolished and not know how to comment.

If a beta really didn't like your book, it is a good idea to try and find out why. I encourage any author to suspend their self-criticism and defensiveness and hear them out. There is a lot to be learned from sincere critical feedback, difficult as it may be. While they're telling you what they didn't like, resist the urge to defend the sections they claim were uninteresting or confusing. You can go back to those sections once you're out of the moment and make your own decisions. Betas are generally not professionals, and it is certain they will not catch everything. Teams of experienced editors make mistakes in professional settings; you can roundly expect your betas to do the same.

Every now and then, you will encounter a genuinely toxic beta reader. These are people who are fundamentally not invested in your success, and who overtly or covertly want to tear you down. There is a huge difference between the feedback you will get from someone who wants you to succeed versus those who do not. The unfortunate thing is that toxic people sometimes claim that they want to help you. They may even be people you consider to be your friends or family.

There are ways to distinguish toxic feedback from useful criticism. Scorn and sarcasm are big giveaways – if the comments on your book are derogatory, self-righteous or snide, put their feedback down and have a talk to them. Challenging your desire to write is something else they often do ("Why did you even bother to write this? It's awful."). Gaslighting, where the reader attempts to convince you of problems you know are not there, is also common. Avoid these people like the plague in your career and personal life.

If someone you know is doing this to you and you consider them your friend, it's time to reassess the relationship. Authors invest much of themselves into their work, and if someone is attacking your work in a way that is neither enlightening or encouraging, they are not being loving towards you.

AFTERMATH

Once your beta readers have gotten back to you, you're ready for your final proofread. If you wrote a query letter or a back-cover blurb and synopsis before you began editing, this is the time to rest your manuscript for a week and work on editing and refining those short, but vital documents. When you're feeling a bit freshened up on the book, you can get into the final stages of preparation: proofing and formatting.

As a final note, remember to ask your proofreaders to read cover copy, titles, and headings, and also to check page numbers. You'd be amazed how often you leave mistakes in such obvious places.

POST-EDITING: PROOFREADING AND FORMATTING

By this point, you would probably be very happy if you never had to read your manuscript again (or, at least, until the damn thing gets published). Unfortunately, most professional writers don't have that luxury. If you do have time for another desk drawer resting period, it may not be a bad idea to set it aside for a month or two before doing the final stages of work. If you have multiple manuscripts, it's definitely a good idea. Rest that sucker after copy editing, and refresh your brain on another project in the meantime. A professional writer is like a chef: they chop vegetables while there's one thing in the oven and something else is cooling on the counter. If you're part of the 1-book-1-month Indie writer crowd, use this period to draft your next book.

The final proofing stage is a pretty mellow exercise compared to the other steps involved in completing a novel. It is fundamentally a hands-off read-aloud of a clean, formatted copy of your manuscript. You can use the PDF reader, but you ideally want a real flesh and blood person to read it aloud for you this time. If you can't find a real person or don't want to show your work to someone else at this stage, a good second option is to record yourself reading it aloud and then play it back, errors included. As you listen to your reader, follow along in the text. You can do this on paper (preferable for most people), PDF (using markup), or your text document file.

At the proofreading stage, you are looking for small, hard-to-spot errors. Common culprits are repeated words ("to to" and "the the" are common), misspellings, wrongly used word substitutes and auto-correct issues. Be alert for paragraphing, formatting errors, wonky line spacing, missing indents and other small details. Pay special attention to chapter headings, titles, headers and footers – it is easy to skip these in your haste.

Once you've been through your manuscript and the final proofing is finished, most of the work is done. Put the work down for a bit and celebrate – you've earned it! And then come crawling back, because the key word in the above sentence is 'most'. Beyond the proofreading phase lies querying, series planning (if you're writing a series), submission, formatting and layout. If you're self-publishing, you have to do ebook and possibly paperback layout, which is an art unto itself and which can take a lot of time if you're not sure how.

The Shunn Manuscript Format is all you need to send your manuscript in to agents and publishers. Advanced formatting is beyond the scope of this guide, but keep an eye out on my Amazon author page for the next books in the *Fix Your Damn Book!* series, aptly titled *Write Your Damn Book!, Format Your Damn Book!* and *Sell Your Damn Book!*

WYDB will cover manuscript formatting, query letter register and formatting, creating tables of contents that work on Kindle and other ebook platforms, ebook formatting, metadata, and paperback layout in Microsoft Word and OpenOffice/LibreOffice. To get notified when it comes out, join my mailing list at: http://eepurl.com/YbEP1.

PUBLISHING TIPS

I'm not really an expert on how to succeed in publishing, beyond what I picked up during my work for magazines and companies over the years and through my own self-publishing endeavors. For more detailed information, I suggest you refer to the real experts: Donald Maass, Holly Lisle, Chuck Wendig, Hugh Howey, Chris Fox, Joanna Penn and others who've been in the legacy and self-publishing industry for years. I've listed the best ones I know, famous and not, in *Appendix D: Resources for Writers*. What I do know has been condensed here for your use.

GET A GOOD COVER

Expect to spend money and time on sourcing a good book cover, if you're self-publishing. If you're not, fight tooth and nail for as good a cover as your publisher can muster.

Self-publishers can expect to spend anywhere from $90 USD for a genre-appropriate, non-exclusive cover design, through to $800 for a professional custom made cover developed in consultation with an expert designer. The money is worth it. Both indie and legacy professionals regard the book cover and the book blurb to be the two most important sales tools of a book, and for good reason.

Screen your designer by asking for a portfolio of their work. Support them by going to a designer only when you have a firm idea what it is you want. If you have no idea what you want, you can't expect someone to make the decision for you. Even if you can't draw, you can research online or in a book store for the kinds of covers you like and create a collage of sorts that you can show to an artist to help them complete something you'll love, and which will help sell more copies of your book.

Genre-appropriateness is more important than depicting anything that is actually in the story. When people are searching for a book, they have subliminally memorized certain visual cues that interest them in a book. Half-naked men on romance novel covers, ¾ action shots and magical effects for urban fantasy, creepy bloody figures on horror books... there's visual tropes for every genre, and you want to meet them.

THE THREE-BOOK THRESHOLD

There is a thing in publishing that is often referred to as the 'three book threshold', or sometimes (if you want to be dramatic) 'the phoenix effect'. The former is more accurate in describing this phenomenon, which amounts to the fact that authors rarely sell many of their first two books, but that around the time the third book in a series comes out, sales pick up. This was true of the magazine I worked with: our subscriptions didn't really get going until the third issue. This is generally because people like to get emotionally invested in novel series and characters, and a single book doesn't guarantee there will be more books in that series. In addition, people generally have short attention spans and enjoy being able to access a large amount of their favorite thing at one time, which they rapidly consume.

If you write in multiple genres or are working on multiple series, finish the first three books of one series before releasing the first of another. Many of the Indie bigshots now recommend that you write the first three books of any series in advance of publication and release them a month apart to leverage the marketplace algorithms that preference books within the first 30 days.

RESEARCH YOUR MARKET

It doesn't matter what your market is, as long as you know something about them. When I first heard this, there was next to no practical advice on the subject, so here's what I know about researching and reaching your market.

You can research your market online and offline. One of the easiest ways is to go on Amazon and Nook and see what's selling well in your genre, Indie and otherwise. Make a list and read the blurbs. The blurbs and covers are the things that tend to sway readers into buying a particular book, though it goes without saying that they should represent the story inside.

Another way to find your market is to Google book bloggers in your genre and see what their websites look like. Read these people and get to know things about them. Also, go on forums that relate to your genre in some way. Science fiction readers can often be found on gaming forums, like Steam. Fantasy readers can often be found on roleplaying boards. Romance readers can be found on a diverse variety of forums depending on the kind of romance you write. Read posts by and get to know people in these locales. Find out what they like. Learn their language, so to speak, and you can tailor your blurbs to that general demographic.

14

COMPETITION AND ORIGINALITY

In the business world, successful competition is a good thing: a sign that there are people who are buying what it is you want to produce and sell. A lot of writers worry that the material they produce isn't original enough, but in reality, every story humans can tell one another has pretty much been told already. Where we can and do express originality is in the execution and the details of voice, setting and character.

It goes without saying that plagiarism is to be avoided at all costs, but don't sweat competition. It means that people want to read what you write. Authors don't really compete in the way that other businesses do – if someone loves a book by one author who writes similarly to you, chances are they will love your book as well. You lose nothing by referring your readers to books you like to read as well. Entertainment is not a zero-sum game, and people are always looking for something to love. Networking with fellow authors is an important and fun exercise which is crucial to getting your books noticed.

PLATFORM

Start a platform early. Use what works for you. It doesn't have to be a blog or a static website: building a community or a reputation on interest forums works just as well. George R.R Martin is known for his presence at the conference circuit, and for a long time, that was his entire platform. These days, some kind of online presence is advisable for authors. Have a look at your favorite authors online and see what they're up to: you can draw inspiration for 'what to do' based on that. Mailing lists are widely acknowledged to be the key marketing tool for authors.

PROMOTION

Have you ever bought a book because someone auto-DM'd you on Twitter? Me neither. Spamming links to your work on social media is not an effective way to advertise it. Neither is kissing up to people for a month, and then dropping off the face of the world in that community once you've made your book known. Sadly, these things are both very common, and neither of them greatly entice people to pick up your work. The root of good promotion is strong networks, which essentially means that you need to hang out with the kinds of people you like and who might also like your work, and share it with them when they want to hear about it.

My experience with Facebook ads has been good, in terms of the return I get in sales. I believe that there's not much point in promoting a novel this way unless you have others in the series due to the cost-return ratio, but it can definitely work.

THE END...?

I really hope you went out and indulged in your vice of choice after finishing your final proofread, because damn, you deserve it! Writing a book is really, really hard, and writing a GOOD book is even harder. After painstakingly editing your manuscript through all of those steps, cleaning and cutting and polishing? There is little doubt in my mind that your book is now in the 'good book' category.

Of course, finishing a manuscript is really only the first step in publication, and may even be the shortest step in the whole process, from idea to book to your rightfully-earned royalties. The period after publication is extraordinarily difficult. If you're not your own best friend, if you self-abuse or succumb to depression, then you will find it very hard to break out. Publishing books is a hard gig, and self-pub isn't any easier than publishing with a house.

I really hope this book helped you, and will continue to help you in your novel-writing adventures. I will be releasing at least two other books in this series: *Sell Your Damn Book!*, which is all about submission, blurb-writing, cover design, formatting and layout, and *Write Your Damn Book!*, which will focus on the outline and drafting process and include strategies for building your books into a series. If you'd like to be notified when those come out, I recommend you join my mailing list or 'Like' my Amazon author page. You can also find me on Facebook.

We've reached the end of the main text, but there

are still the appendices to go. These contain info intended to help you beyond your editorial adventures, and look into four big topics that don't really fit into other places in this guide: query letters and back-cover blurbs, software for writers and editors, editing to strengthen and un-objectify female characters, and resources and further reading for authors.

I also invite you to contact me with a bit about yourself and your book, and to chat about the trials and tribulations of writing and editing. You can email me at: author@jamesosiris.com.

If you enjoyed this book and are willing to leave a quick review on that would be brilliant. You can do that by visiting: https://amzn.com/B01FQOI1P0 Shout-outs on Facebook are also super helpful.

Thanks for reading, and happy editing!

APPENDIX A: THE DREAD QUERY

Query letters are the bane of most author's lives, and the process of writing and refining them is one of the most fraught parts of working on a book. I included this appendix because it ties into the Plot Planner/Ideal Synopsis phase of editing. I know that a lot of writers save the query until after they've finished everything, but it really helps to have a blurb before you get stuck into writing a book, let alone the dedicated developmental editing stage.

A query letter is basically the same as a back-cover blurb: a snappy 100 to 200-word summary of your novel which offers the first tantalizing hints of suspense. The difference between a query letter and a back cover blurb is that a query is a business letter, and a blurb is a marketing tool without the need for extra business fluff. The blurb goes into the query as the 'pitch'.

The elements of writing and submitting query letters will be treated at more length in my other books, Write Your Damn Book! and Publish Your Damn Book! This appendix is really to assist you with any queries you may have drafted, and also to get you thinking about the elements of a query if you haven't yet written one.

Queries have a format. The format can usually be

boiled down to a kind of equation, which is as follows:

[NOVEL TITLE] is about [Protagonist], an [interesting professional or person] who is drawn into [a series of cascading events] which will bring about [some bad thing] if they don't intervene.

Now, of course, your blurb is going to look a lot more sophisticated than this. But when you're drafting, this is what you need. Someone capable of doing something, the circumstances in which they are doing it, and the stakes that they are doing it for. The question of the stakes creates suspense. Suspense creates the desire to read the book.

When you're editing your query, you need to look for some specific elements and address some specific questions.

Elements

- Find a good adjective to describe your hero. Find another one to describe the primary antagonist. Surly, determined, insightful, idealistic... whatever works for your characters. You can use an adverb or adjective here, because blurbs have to be short.

- A compelling goal which inspires some kind of emotion. Anything relating to food, violence, sex or chaos is inclined to stimulate emotions at the base level. The most compelling emotion to evoke in writing is anger, so if you can include a bit of outrage, give it a try.

- End on a suspenseful note. You want to leave the outcome of the story uncertain when you're writing a blurb.

Common problems that occur in blurbs/queries include:

- Too long. Keep it well under 200 words.

- Too opaque. Don't try to be mysterious or vague in an effort to create suspense. Lay out an action that needs to be taken, and then leave the outcome of the action uncertain. "Three commandos are sent to rescue a missing soldier, the last of three brothers, who is missing in action on the chaotic battlefields of Nazi-occupied France." The suspense is implied by the unresolved action – can they find him? You don't need to be obtuse to create suspense.

- Too complex: queries shouldn't involve your subplots. Cut to the heart of the story and leave the outcome uncertain.

You will need to study blurbs in your genre to get a sense of the formula that you need – and in all genres, fiction and non-fiction, there is a rough formula for every blurb. To understand how suspense works, I highly recommend that you study the blurbs of thrillers and crime dramas. They are genres which use suspense to sell, and their blurbs have to be particularly trim and punchy. Even authors of cozy mysteries and regency romance can learn a great deal from the likes of Dan Brown, Sara Paretsky, and Michael Crichton.

Another great resource that you can find online is Query Shark. Be warned, this site is very snarky, sometimes to the point of derision. Even so, there's a lot of good lessons to be learned from those who are critiqued by the resident literary agent.

APPENDIX B: SOFTWARE FOR WRITING AND EDITING

What is the best software for writers? This is a question many writers ask, but there's not One Magic Program to Rule Them All. Individual preference is the biggest factor when it comes to software for drafting, refining, formatting and publishing a book. George R.R Martin famously uses the ancient DOS program WordStar. Other writers, like Stephen King, often draft parts of their novels by hand.

You probably don't have a DOS machine from the 80's, but fortunately, there are now many software programs for writers. The following is a list of my favorites and those that come recommended by writers from around the web.

DRAFTING

My opinion is that good old fashioned pen and paper is hard to beat for notes, sketching, and ideas. However, there are some contenders for those whippersnapper young'uns who don't like handwriting.

FocusWriter (all platforms, including Linux)

FocusWriter is my personal favorite digital drafting tool. I do my first drafts by hand, and 'type in' with this program. It is an easy-to-use, reliable and attractive program which offers a full-screen/distraction-free writing environment. You can easily customize font, background, formatting and text area width, as well as set word count or duration goals. It's also free, or you can donate to the program author.

WriteRoom (Mac) and Byword (Mac)

These are Mac-specific 'distraction-free' writing tools. WriteRoom is very similar to FocusWriter. It is fairly basic full-screen/distraction-free writing software that allows for quicker and more focused drafting. Byword is a bit fancier and supports Markdown. It features Mac keyboard shortcuts, word counters with live updates, and syncing across devices.

Write or Die

Some people swear by this program, while others hate it for its extensive 'bells and whistles' approach. Most writing programs rely on your innate sense of self-discipline to be effective: Write or Die bribes, cajoles or rewards you to write. It offers a 'punishment' mode that will play horrible sounds and images, a 'stimulus' mode to woo you into writing for longer, and a 'kamikaze' mode that will actually start unwriting your words if you take a break or stop. Pretty intense.

Write or Die is a bit like a steampunk writer's tomato timer, except that instead of getting a neutral 'bing!' every 20 minutes, you get kittens and purring as your reward, or alarms and spiders as punishment. As writing programs go, this one looks and feels a bit like a slot machine. As I said, some people love it. If you find discipline to be a problem and also enjoy a bit of competition, it might be right up your alley. You can try it for free, but the full version costs $20 USD.

COMPILING, REVISING, AND STRUCTURING

Scrivener

Scrivener is THE quintessential writer's software, in many ways. It is good for any stage of the writing process, but I find that it excels at sorting out messy first drafts. This is the program I recommend you use to get your book into shape.

Scrivener has so many features that it is hard to list them all. A corkboard with index cards, individual chapters, dual windows (so you can look at an old draft and revise a new draft in another panel), chapter management, editing tools, story generation tools, formatting and draft compiling tools, backup and draft management... this baby has everything. Because of this, it also has quite a learning curve – but if you want to run with the pros, Scrivener is what you want.

I personally find that Scrivener isn't as good as Microsoft Word for formatting. You could probably use it for this purpose, but it would be difficult.

Scrivener only costs $40 USD, and there is usually a steep discount for NaNoWriMo winners every year. There's a 30-day free trial period and lots of testimonials from published authors who wrote their books (in whole or in part) in Scrivener.

LibreOffice Writer

LibreOffice (and OpenOffice) are both very similar programs. They work somewhat like older Windows XP-style versions of Microsoft Office, before Microsoft got carried away with ribbon navigation and fancy-schmancy XML. It's free, comprehensive, and doesn't have many bells and whistles. Its files are also highly compatible with Microsoft Office programs. Given that Microsoft Office is standard in the publishing industry, it's good to have some assurance that your manuscript will look the same on the Penguin Acquisitions Editor's screen as it does on yours.

Save the Cat! Story Structure Software

The late Blake Snyder's 'Save the Cat!' series is to screenwriting what Stephen King's 'On Writing' is for novelists: an absolute treasure trove of information, hacks and advice on how to write a screenplay or movie script. Much of the advice in Save the Cat! is also applicable to authors writing books, especially if you're just starting out and wondering how to write a novel.

The company that Blake started now publishes writing software based on *Save the Cat!*, which retails for $99.95 on their website. I have never tried it, but if you're a fan of the books and want to pump out commercial novels or screenplays, it could be everything you ever wanted.

Snowflake Pro

Another reasonably pricey bit of software, Snowflake Pro is based on Randy Ingermanson's 'Snowflake Method' of novel planning and writing. It is probably most suited to die-hard plotters – not so much for pantsing.

EDITING

There's not really any good comprehensive editing software out there, I'm afraid. The grammar checkers in Word and LibreOffice are about the best you're going to find for copy editing, and they are still pretty awful. Grammarly and programs like it are expensive and have a lot of limitations. Personally, I wouldn't bother.

One program that does deserve a mention is the Hemmingway App. Hemingway is an automated grammar checker which looks for a few specific problems: run-on sentences, passive voice, complex or obscure words, and adverbs.

However, Hemingway is still kind of basic. It cannot recognize rhetorical devices, for example. It will mark up good sentences that sound beautiful to the ear as being 'too complex', and it will falsely identify passive voice. It will point out every adverb you use, but it can't recognize 'weak' words like 'might', 'could' and 'should'. For example, the sentences below are from some terrible roleplaying I saw, but they pass Hemingway's 'tests':

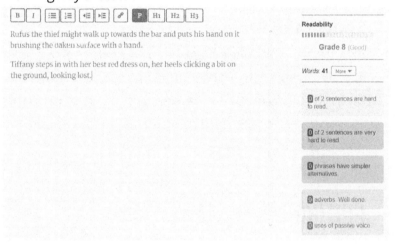

If you recognize the limitations of this app and use it carefully, Hemingway can be useful at the copy editing stage of writing. It's possibly even more useful for non-fiction, where short sentences and clarity are both desirable.

FORMATTING

Sigil

If you are compiling an ebook, Sigil is an excellent program. It is free, simple to use, and creates very nice, functional ebooks suitable for Kindle, Kobo, B&N and Smashwords. The spelling, grammar and formatting functions are very limited. I would not advise drafting or correcting your drafts in Sigil.

When you paste Word/Scrivener/OpenOffice-formatted content into Sigil, Sigil strips it down to plain text and converts everything to XML. This means that, if you correct or change something in Sigil and paste it back into your other writing program, it does strange things to the formatting which can be finicky to correct. This is a last-stage ebook creation program only.

APPENDIX C:
DEVELOPMENTAL EDITING TO ADDRESS SEXISM

I'm saddened that, as of 2016, readers, editors and authors still have to talk about the way that women (and LGBT people, and people who are not Anglo-Saxon) are treated in fiction. I'd prefer that this issue didn't have to be treated separately (or treated at all) but that's how things are in the world.

Things are getting better, especially in the realm of Young Adult/New Adult fiction, but there are still problems. What problems? Sexual objectification at the expense of substance is still a big one. Shallow characterization, sidelining, romanticization of abuse, the use of rape as a male hero-centric plot device, and the *defense* of these things by certain sections of the community... these are all symptoms of a society recovering from the days when the word 'sexism' hadn't been coined, and women (and minorities) simply didn't have the language to describe what was happening to them.

In addition to the ethics of addressing sexism, there is a bottom-line incentive for authors to think about. Women are now the majority market for both novels and video games (yes, really: the Internet Advertising Bureau found that 52 percent of all gamers are now women, and most of them play on PC/console, not mobile). Seventy-five percent of all novel readers are women over 30. Alienating three-quarters of your potential market because you decided to stick your hero's dismembered girlfriend in a freezer to motivate him is not going to be a great sales tactic in the near future.

The material in this appendix is also good for any character in your book that might seem 'off' or superfluous to you somehow. In line with the advice in the developmental editing section, consider whether or not characters who seem to have little or no purpose really need to be in the novel.

The major developmental problems related to sexism that I encounter in manuscripts can be summarized as *objectification, sidelining, and exploitation.* This handy checklist, written by Tasha Robinson of *The Dissolve*, is great for screening any character for these things. The original list and accompanying (amazing) article can be found at: http://thedissolve.com/features/exposition/618-were-losing-all-our-strong-female-characters-to-tr/

1. *After being introduced, does your Strong Female Character then fail to do anything fundamentally significant to the outcome of the plot?*

2. *If she does accomplish something plot-significant, is it primarily getting raped, beaten, or killed to motivate a male hero? Or deciding to have sex with/not have sex with/agreeing to date/deciding to break up with a male hero? Or nagging a male hero into growing up, or nagging him to stop being so heroic? Basically, does she only exist to service the male hero's needs, development, or motivations?*

3. *Could your Strong Female Character be seamlessly replaced with a floor lamp with some useful information written on it to help a male hero?*

4. *Is a fundamental point of your plot that your Strong Female Character is the strongest, smartest, meanest, toughest, or most experienced character in the story – until the protagonist arrives?*

5. *...or worse, does he enter the story as a bumbling fuck-up, but spend the whole movie rapidly evolving past her, while she stays entirely static, and even cheers him on?*

6. *Does your Strong Female Character exist primarily so the protagonist can impress her?*

7. *It's nice if she's hyper-cool, but does she only start off that way so a male hero will look even cooler by comparison when he rescues or surpasses her?*

8. *Is she so strong and capable that she's never needed rescuing before now, but once the plot kicks into gear, she's suddenly captured or*

FIX YOUR DAMN BOOK!

*threatened by the villain, and needs the hero's
intervention? Is breaking down her pride a
fundamental part of the story?*

9. *Does she disappear entirely for the second
half/third act of the film, for any reason other
than because she's doing something significant to
the plot (besides being a hostage, or dying)?*

I would also add:

10. Is your female character unnecessarily child-
like in appearance or behavior? Is she
infantilized at any point?

11. Is her entire reason for being in the story
related to her feelings or desire for a man?

12. Does she spend an inordinate amount of time
sick or unconscious despite being typed as
strong/powerful? This is a pretty sure-fire
indication that she's been removed from the
plot, and has become an object with no agency
of her own.

13. Do you, the author, spend considerably more
time describing her appearance relative to
your male characters?

14. Does her costume consist entirely of modified
underwear, when her role is not the kind of
role where people generally run around in
lingerie?

Now, if you go through this list and answer in the
affirmative to some or all of these points – and
assuming you are a socially conscious individual who

doesn't mean (or want) to buy into tired old stereotypes about women – how do you fix them?

- If your female characters pull a vanishing act in the second half of the story, consider merging one of the male characters who does play a part into her and having them be the one female character instead of two separate bit-players.
- If you identify a female character (or characters) without a strong arc, give them one.
- A strong story arc includes well-rounded strengths and weaknesses.
- Examine dialogue for clues as to your female character's motivations. Are they all about love, sex and/or self-pity? If so, pick an alternative motivation and write it in.
- If your female character starts off being cool and tough, have her remain so for the duration of the story. Don't 'uncool' her because it suits the needs of a male protagonist.
- If she is childlike or infantilized without good reason, give her some real agency. If you're writing a period or fantasy story with a character who has been sheltered, give her a good reason and opportunity to grow up. Arya and Sansa Stark from *A Game of Thrones* both had pretty sheltered lives which diverged in some seriously different ways. There's opportunity there.
- The time and setting of a story is no reason to glorify the nasty shit that happened to women back in the day. Glorification occurs when there is excessive emphasis put on a behavior which is

done over and over in the course of a story. Just because you're writing a fantasy setting that is based on medieval times doesn't mean that your female characters have to be objectified plot devices used to motivate a male protagonist.

- Yes, rape is a real problem that women face. Yes, women with agency tend to be threatened sexually more often than men. But if we're reading a novel, we are looking for protagonists who are protagging. If your female characters have enough agency to be involved in the plot, they have enough agency to avoid being knocked out/drugged/assaulted/poisoned so that the male hero can save them.

- Giving a character agency doesn't necessarily mean turning them into men. It means giving them opinions, ability, and a reason to be in the plot.

- Remove disempowering stereotypes. Be particularly alert to combination sex and race stereotypes. If you're not sure whether you've subscribed to a stereotype, go look them up on the TV Tropes website and see what you can find. This is also true of LGBTI stereotypes and racial stereotypes as well. Even if you think some of these stereotypes are flattering from your perspective, they may not be flattering to the people who have to live with these socially assigned badges of identity day in, day out.

- Butch women are fine. Femme women are fine. Women who relate to their biological sex, but question their gender are fine. Transgender women are fine. There is no one female experience, no more than there is any one male experience.

The treatment of sexual violence in fiction is a hotly contested topic and is one on which there is currently little consensus. I am personally of the opinion that these stories should not be erased from our stories, because victims of sexual assault are frequently erased, ignored or blamed outside of books and I don't believe that their stories should be removed from fiction as well. However, some care must be taken when dealing with the subject. Unlike other forms of violence that we accept in fiction – revenge, self-defense, action hero/ine body-counts for a higher cause – sexual assault is fundamentally the exercise of power by the powerful over the disempowered. It is often normalized and taken for granted, and the act of being victimized is frequently pinned on the victim, not the perpetrator. This is true for male victims as well as female victims.

By disempowering any character this way, you remove their ability to protag - their only recourse after being subject to sexual violence in the course of a story is one of Stockholm Syndrome, recovery, or revenge. Instead of becoming actors, they are relegated to the role of 'reactors'. They spend time picking up the pieces of themselves when they could be doing other things.

If you're looking to understand the dynamics of power that operate in and around women, I highly recommend you read *What I learned from dating women who have been raped* by Emma Lindsey. She skillfully captures the experience of everyday powerlessness that many women (and gay people, and trans people) feel, and also the ways that powerlessness is taken for granted by both perpetrator and victim. You can find the article on Medium: https://medium.com/@emmalindsay/what-i-learned-from-dating-women-who-have-been-raped-583e1001b6cd#.1lw7wle1c

That's pretty much it. If you disagree, it's no skin off my back, but remember this: no matter what your politics happens to be, the stories we tell one another are the stories which are heard and remembered.

So whose story do *you* want to tell?

APPENDIX D: RESOURCES FOR WRITERS & EDITORS

These are the other books I have read myself and recommend to other writers and editors. They span writing, psychology, editing and the business of selling books. The links will take you to the Amazon sales page.

Every one of these books are my highest recommended reads for improving your craft. They informed a dramatic improvement in my own work, and have also transformed the work of other writers I know. I've listed them in order of value.

Techniques of the Selling Writer by Dwight V Swain

As discussed earlier in the book, this is one of the best practical guides to writing I have ever read. Every paragraph has something to offer.

Link: http://bit.ly/dwightvswain

Write to Market: Deliver a Book That

Sells by Chris Fox

This is an excellent, snappy, informative book written by one of the best breakout authors in the Indie world right now. Highly recommended for those who take self-publishing seriously.
Link: http://bit.ly/CFox_W2M

The Writer's Book of Hope by Ralph Keyes

An incredible little book to help you feel more positive and hopeful about your work. Ralph Keyes is a very inspiring writer, and this book contains much-needed wisdom for those of us flailing around in the slush pile.
Link: http://amzn.to/1Q6qMBS

Save the Cat by Blake Snyder

The screenwriter's bible, *Save the Cat* is a really fun, practical, useful book. All of the advice in this book is applicable to novelists. This is the book that taught me how to write loglines and queries that hook people – and actually, how to write hooks at all.
Link: http://amzn.to/1XCBcuk

Writing the Breakout Novel by Donald Maass

A book written by one of the most venerable and sought-after agents in the New York publishing scene, Donald Maass has a lot of valuable advice for authors: those starting out, and those who are mid-career. It is, however, very 'high pressure'. Agents want bestsellers,

after all.
Link: http://amzn.to/20JYOgK

On Writing: A Memoir of the Craft by Stephen King

A very well-known book and an excellent entry into the writer's story. Like him or hate him, Stephen King is a self-made man and has a lot to offer other writers, which he does generously and with great compassion in this book.
Link: http://bit.ly/onwritingSK

SPIN Selling by Neil Rackham

SPIN Selling is *the* book on sales – despite the rather cheesy name, this book is genuine, practical, and will teach you the art of the deal. The content of this book is not directly related to writing fiction, but it is very applicable during all stages of submission, publishing, promotion, and negotiation. It's also generally good business advice for those of us who regard writing as our career, and lays out highly effective techniques for ethical marketing.
Link: http://amzn.to/1WwPMm0

The Plot Whisperer: Secrets of Story Structure Any Writer Can Master by Martha Alderson

A really excellent book on structure that is likely to

appeal to the pantsers among you. Martha Alderson presents a very practical and easy-to-follow guide on structuring coherent plots.

Link: http://amzn.to/1UcUAyp

Invisible Ink by Brian McDonald

If you struggle with the question: "What is my book really about?", then you need this book. Brian McDonald presents an extremely insightful method on how to get to the heart of your book and define its soul.

Link: http://amzn.to/1QqZFx6

From 2K to 10K: Writing Faster, Writing Better, And Writing More of What You Love by Rachel Aaron

An excellent, if short guide on how to increase your writing output.

Link: http://amzn.to/1Q6rqPJ

First Draft in 30 Days: A Novel Writer's System for Building a Complete and Cohesive Manuscript

If you ever wanted to learn how to outline, this book is for you. It is replete with good structuring advice, though some people may find it a bit pedantic.

Link: http://amzn.to/1RTqak4

The Art of Asking: How I Learned to Stop Worrying and Let People Help by Amanda Palmer

Amanda Palmer began her career as a street performer. This is a very beautiful and sensitive book, partly autobiographical, with information on collaborating, promoting and sharing with other creatives. Very useful for those wondering how to become comfortable with promoting your own work.
Link: http://amzn.to/20JXHh3

Rivet your readers with deep point of view by Jill Elizabeth Nelson

A great little guide to third-person intimate perspective, and how to write it. If you Enjoy that particular POV and want to master it, this comes highly recommended. I used to waver between omniscient and intimate quite a lot before reading this.
Link: http://amzn.to/1Kw5mxM

The First 50 Pages by Jeff Gerke

This book can be snappy and a little acerbic at times, but it is a fun read and an extremely good read for people who want to land an agent or publisher.
Link: http://amzn.to/1XCCsOL

Self-editing on a penny by Ashlyn Forge

Another Indie guide to self-editing, Ashlyn has been

turning out books of exceptional quality for years. Whatever this book lacks, her book probably has.
Link: http://amzn.to/1mMX20V

Buzzmarketing: Get people to talk about your stuff

Another marketing/promotional book that is quite relevant to authors, and which is written in a way to be friendly to those of us who are not naturally very 'markety'.
Link: http://amzn.to/1XCCGoC

Let's get visible by David Gaughran

Surely one of the best guides to self-publishing ever released. David Gaughran teaches you everything you ever wanted to know about publishing on Kindle. It can be quite technical, but it's very good.
Link: http://amzn.to/1SFJVg1

The Personal MBA by Josh Kaufman

If you're hoping to run your writing as a business, you need to know what you're doing. This is an excellent book on business operations, and if you want to learn how to market, sell and manage a writing business, this is an excellent place to start.
Link: http://amzn.to/1OkmYHC

FIND MY FICTION

If Russian wizard hitmages and/or tragic military sci-fi sounds like your deal, check out my fiction titles:

BLOOD HOUND (ALEXI SOKOLSKY #1)

"My name is Alexi Sokolsky: blood mage, occult scholar, and hired killer. Three things that should convey me some immunity in the dog-eat-dog world of the Russian mafia.

Fat chance. In reality, I think too much, drink too little, and if there's one thing the underworld teaches you, it's that there's always a shark bigger and hungrier than you.

Life gets tough after a man turns up dead in our territory, his mutilated body scrawled with demonic sigils. It gets tougher when a key ally of my Organization is kidnapped by a secretive death cult... and I'm the errand boy sent to hunt them down and bring him back.

Then I get captured, nearly killed, and am immersed in a sea of cosmic horror the likes of which I've never known. The stakes are nothing less than the daughter of GOD Itself... and she's calling to me for help.

My name is Alexi Sokolsky: blood mage, occult scholar, hired killer... and hapless pawn in the great game between Everything and the NO-thing trying to destroy it."

Get it here: http://amzn.to/1Qaxc4H

GOD HAS HEARD (LILIUM 1)

When God is used as a weapon, nothing is sacred.

The Samuel-226 PatriotRangers are one of the most successful units in the Holy Legion of the UNAC. They have never lost a man, until one of their brothers, Twofer, disappears during a training exercise. The Host, self-proclaimed reincarnations of Christ, tell them that Twofer has been Saved and taken to Yetzirah, the promised land of the Nephilim.

This, like many things the Host tells its slaves, is a lie.

The leader of Samuel-226, Alpha, becomes obsessed with finding his missing soldier. Without his leadership, his lover and medic, Mike, fights to hold the squad together as it is wracked by conspiracy and fear. As the horrific truth unfolds, the squad begins to question everything they know... but as Mike soon learns, just knowing the truth is a revolutionary act, and God is always listening.

God Has Heard is military science-fiction: a dark war story of martyrdom and ultimate triumph, brotherhood and dignity in the face of total oppression. With echoes of 1984 and Saving Private Ryan, it is a short, intense, thought-provoking read.

Get it here: http://amzn.to/1n0IR8H

ABOUT THE AUTHOR

James Osiris Baldwin is the former Contributing Editor of the Australian Journal of Dementia Care, a published author, and potty-mouthed pioneer in helping Indie authors master their craft. When not quibbling over commas, he works on a range of 'arcane noir' urban fantasy novels.

HIRE ME!

If you're interested in hiring me as your editor, get in touch with me at my business email address and tell me a bit about yourself, your project, and send the first three chapters of your book (in doc or docx format). My price list and rates are public, and are available at: http://jamesosiris.com/book-editing-services/

I offer a free sample 10-page sample edit and a 15-30 minute project consultation (via Skype) on request.

My rates are negotiable within reason (based on your circumstances and my workload), but serious inquiries only, please.